SACRED GEOMETRY HEALING WATER

How you can make it for greater Health, Immune System, and Longevity

By: Michael D. Miller

Table of Contents

Chapter One

The author's story:

In 1968 I was twenty-eight years-old. I was a captain in the US Army. I was sent to fight in the Vietnam War that was raging at that time.

As most young American men did, I focused on doing my duty to my country. As God would have it, I was placed in dangerous situations. It didn't look as if I would return home to my wife and young son. As young men have done for thousands of years when placed in this same situation, I plunged ahead and did my duty. But I was vaguely aware that this force that I had always been told was "God" was somehow in charge of all this. Then, when my year in combat was over, I was somewhat amazed to see that I was still alive. Wow, did I have some close calls!

Again, I had this vaguely tantalizing knowing that this force known as God, having placed me in the path of certain destruction, had also arranged it so that I survived and would get to go home to my family. That I had survived was illogical. Simply put, I should not have made it. So what was going on???

Years later I began to ponder on all this. I will not bore you with the details, but I was then launched into a quest for knowledge about what I had experienced in Vietnam. I spent years reading and researching. The result was that I finally accepted that God was real. This led me to spend the rest of my life reading and studying about Him, searching for his many truths.

This book is the result of some of this searching.

What I have learned is that there is certain esoteric and hidden knowledge that can be found and learned by anyone. But, paradoxically, few seek out and learn this knowledge. You have chosen to read this book. Thus you may be one of those special people, the special people who can handle and properly use this knowledge. It is for you that this book was written.

With this knowledge you will use simple universal truths to turn your ordinary household water into a healing water that will enhance the health, longevity, and emotional well-being of you and your family. I find this exciting!

Chapter Two

Learning about Sacred Geometry

Way back in 1976 my dad gave me a book titled "Pyramid Power". He was fascinated with this book. So I read the book. Now, some thirty years later, I can still recall clearly one of the things mentioned in the book: {If a dull razor blade is suspended in a small pyramid that has the same proportional dimensions as the Great Pyramid of Giza, and is suspended one third down from the apex of the pyramid, it will become sharp again. Likewise, if fresh fruit is placed at the same spot, it will never spoil.}

So this improbable bit of information stuck in my mind. But I was never interested enough to pursue the matter further.

Then in 2008 my wife asked me to go to Egypt with her to attend a Rosicrucian tour of the great temples of Egypt. Reluctantly I went. I had little fascination for visiting the Middle East.

The two-week tour changed my life. I experienced some things during the tour that were inexplicable.

First of all, one early morning we visited the temple of Karnack at Luxor. During the tour, I entered a small chamber that contained a 5,000 year-old life-size statue of the Egyptian Goddess Sekhmet. I was totally unprepared for what I experienced. I was overwhelmed by a wonderful feeling of love and happiness. I glanced at the blue-green marble statue at the end of the chamber, wondering what-in-the-heck was happening to me. A picture of this statue is enclosed.

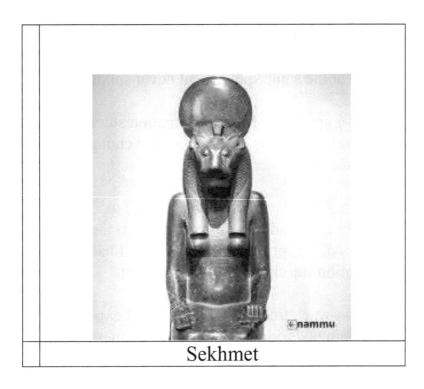

Sekhmet

As I stood there for several minutes, the overwhelming energy of love began to overcome me. I panicked and fled the chamber. Later several friends commented to me that I looked "stricken" when I exited the chamber. They were right, although I didn't tell them why.

Then a week or so later we visited the Great Pyramid at Giza. By special invitation we were allowed to enter the King's Chamber. Many tourists visit the Great Pyramid. Thousands daily, actually. From all over the world.

As I stood in the King's Chamber I felt good. The place had a gentle, pleasing presence. The room was bare. No hieroglyphics of any type. All other monuments and temples we visited had been completely covered with hieroglyphics. At one end stood an open red marble box. It resembled on open coffin, and had no lid. It was referred to as a sarcophagus, but I did not believe that is what it was. [A sarcophagus is a stone box into which a king's coffin is placed for safe-keeping].

Some people were crawling into the red stone box to experience what it felt like. I joined the line of people waiting to do this. I crawled into the stone box (it stood about 4 feet high). As I lay back, I was hit with an amazing surge of energy. I wanted to lay there longer, but other people were waiting behind me to have this experience. My best guess is that I was in the box for about 2 minutes.

That two minutes changed my life. During that two minutes I was placed in a position within the red marble box so that all of the tremendous energy created by the perfect symmetry of the millions of tons of marble and granite stone of the perfect pyramid was focused on my heart and aura. Just as a dulled razor blade was perfected by being exposed to the energies of the powers of that special spot in the Great Pyramid.

As further research revealed to me, I had been given a rare opportunity to personally experience the sacred geometry of the Great Pyramid. What had been revealed to me was that:

1. There are certain geometric shapes that gather and concentrate harmonic and beneficial natural energies of the universe. Some ancient civilizations knew this and knew how to harness these energies. We are now rediscovering these secrets.

2. By learning this knowledge, and by capturing these beneficial energies of the universe, we can improve our lives. We can design our homes, enrich our water and food, improve our health, and have greater peace of mind and wellbeing.

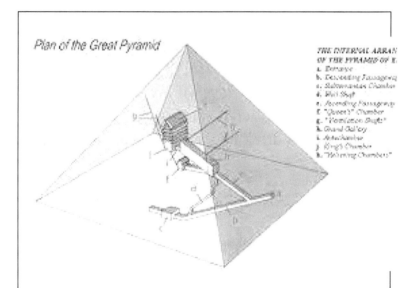

Plan of the Great Pyramid

A view of the location of the King's Chamber. It is directly below the apex of the pyramid, thus collecting all of the pyramid's focused energy.

Chapter Three

How I use Sacred Geometry to make healing water

Each person has an energy level. In general, the higher your energy level, the more healthy you are, the more energy you have and the more stamina you possess. We drink a lot of water each day. My healing method simply involves increasing the energy level of the water that we drink, which will increase our body's energy levels.

I increase the energy level of my water by using the principles of sacred geometry to energize my water before I drink it.

My Concentric Cylinders Method

We have briefly looked at the power of the sacred pyramid to generate universal energy. Another of the most powerful geometric shapes that gathers harmonious and beneficial energies from the universe is the circle. Extended in three dimensions, the circle becomes a cylinder. A cylinder collects beneficial energies. Placed in a cylinder, water will accumulate the powerful and beneficial energies that we seek.

I have found that the best design is a series of cylinders as shown in the below picture. However, the best layout appears to be three concentric cylinders. Briefly, it takes 5 days to energize a bottle of water in one cylinder. This period is shortened to 3 days when three concentric cylinders are used. So I recommend 3 cylinders.

I have used various materials for my cylinders; cans, tubes, etc... The picture shows mailing tubes. They can be ordered on the Internet. I use mailing tubes 12 inches high, custom cut for me by the mailing tube company.

The picture shows me using three concentric cylinders. I have learned that three concentric cylinders is optimum. So now all of my systems use three cylinders. In the picture are shown 12 inch tall mailing tubes of 5 inches, 6 inches and 8 inches diameter, all stacked together. I have glued small cork spacers between them to keep their spacing fixed.

3 Days in my sacred geometry collector tubes
will energize this water.

The seedlings on the right were watered with tap water. The seedlings on the left were watered with Sacred Geometry Healing Water.

This picture is worth ten thousand words!

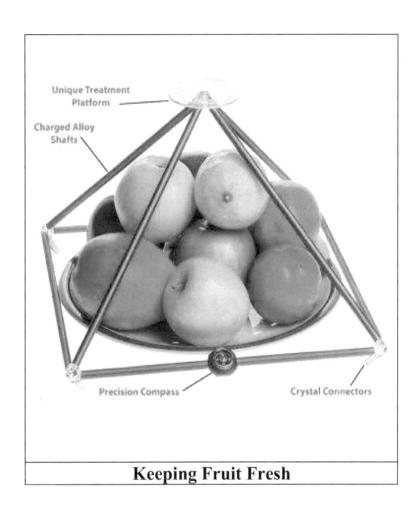

Unique Treatment Platform

Charged Alloy Shafts

Precision Compass

Crystal Connectors

Keeping Fruit Fresh

The Pyramid Energy Method

Another method of energizing your drinking water is to simply place a container of water under a pyramid, similar to the picture of fruit being placed under a pyramid to be kept fresh (picture is above). Three days seems to be an optimum time to energize the water.

In this regard it is important that your pyramid have the proper dimensions. It must have the same proportions as the Great Pyramid of Giza. The actual dimensions of the pyramid are 440 cubits for each base, 280 cubits high, and 418 cubits for each of the four arms reaching from each corner of the base to the top. It is critical that your pyramid have arms as shown on the below drawing that are .95 of the length of each base.

To energize water, I use a pyramid that has exactly 20 5/8 inches as a base length (this is a Royal Cubit). The Royal Cubit is said to also be a sacred geometry length of measure, and has its own source of power. Thus by building my sacred geometry pyramid that has the special proportions of the Great Pyramid dimensions, and also has a

Royal Cubit length, I am making a pyramid that really has super powers. My dimensions are a base of 20 5/8 inches and an arm length of 19.6 inches.

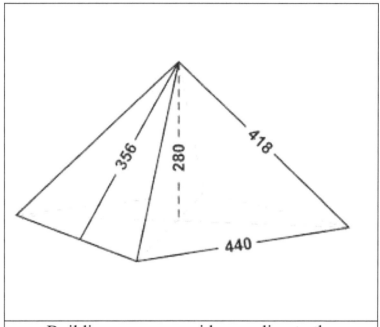

Building your pyramid according to the proportions of the Great Pyramid is critical. A royal cubit is 20 5/8 inches.

What kind of pyramid to use. It has become fashionable to build pyramids that are simple frames of the basic dimensions. Here is what one looks like.

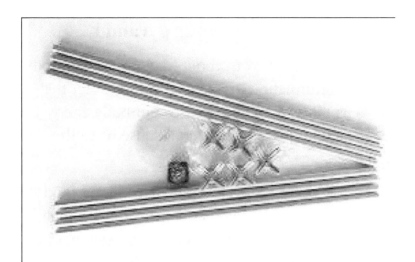

Pyramid kits sold by Nick Edwards and others online are cheap and effective….

To make a pyramid like this. This is what I use.

How to use your pyramid

Now I wish to tell you about how my friends and I use this information to make a healing water that gives us more energy, increases our body energy levels and improves our overall sense of well-being.

1. My setup: I have a shelf space in my food pantry room that is approximately 16 inches by 36 inches. I have fitted eight sets of three concentric ring cylinders in this space. I place a used 1.5 liter glass wine bottle, filled with filtered water, in each cylinder. After 3 days it is ready to drink. I make my coffee with it, and use it as my drinking and cooking water.

2. I have a friend who has suspended a 15 inch tubular pyramid from the ceiling of his pantry. He places 1 gallon plastic water bottles on the floor, under the pyramid. He also uses this water for his house plants and claims fantastic results with his plants.

3. Another friend keeps a 12 inch pyramid on his kitchen counter. He places containers of water under the pyramid, as uses it as needed.

4. Several people have suspended pyramids of various sizes over their beds or office desks. They report greater alertness at their desks, and greater relaxation when they sleep. I use this method. It really keeps me alert when I am sleepy and need to do some office work.

5. One guy has hung a pyramid from his bathroom ceiling, directly over where he stores his razor. He uses it to keep his disposable razor sharp. He claims that each disposable razor used to last him a week. Now it lasts him six months. He brags that his shaving cost savings have paid for all of the costs of making and installing his sacred energy devices.

6. With a little imagination you will probably come up with more imaginative ways to use these sacred geometry energy systems. Go for it!

| Hey, don't laugh! This works, giving a deeper level of meditation. | Or you can go bigger! |

Chapter Four
Combining Water Energizing Systems

There are some fantastic books out there that tell great wisdom about sacred geometry. At the end of this booklet we list a bibliography that has aided our research greatly.

In the course of our work we also discovered that a few great people have also made significant discoveries in developing ways to make water and wonderful healing and anti-aging element. We shall now discuss the most important of these discoveries.

Viktor Schauberger
And his discoveries about water

In Austria, back in the 1930s, a young forest warden by the name of Viktor Schauberger made some startling observations. He noticed that trout in a fast moving mountain stream were able to dart about at fast speeds that could not be explained by the movement of their fins alone. He concluded that the tumbling and spinning of the fast moving mountain streams imparted an energy to the fish that allowed for their fast movement. Using this knowledge, he became famous for his ability to manipulate water for large successful water projects. He also demonstrated that water energized by tumbling and spinning down a mountain stream had distinctive health benefits. Crops grew better and animals and people were healthier when they drank this water.

He became famous. When Germany took over Austria, Schauberger was forced by the Nazis to set up a laboratory to further his developments. He made some amazing scientific discoveries about the ability of "structured" water to generate energy and power.

At the end of WWII the American Army forcibly placed Schauberger in a remote military base in South Texas where they replicated his experiments. He remained there until just before he died ten years later. His discoveries about the structure of water have never been made public. However a fascinating book, "Living Energies" by Callum Coates is available on amazon.com and it finally reveals much about this fascinating man and his work to structure water to benefit mankind.

In the 1980s a chemist, Jim Sheridan, working for the Dow Chemical Company in Midland, Michigan, decided to seek a chemical cure for cancer. Working alone, and on his spare time, he made considerable progress. But he was consistently thwarted by his inability to get governmental approvals for his work. Eventually he brought in another friend to assist him named Ed Sopcak. Ed was an electrical engineer. Unable to make Jim's method work, Ed undertook another approach. He sought an electrical approach. Eventually he was successful, and they developed a liquid that they called Cancell.

To avoid problems with the government, they decided to give their healing liquid away for free. They set up a separate telephone line to receive orders. I attempted to place an order as soon as I heard about this. But the line was always busy. Apparently business was good! Eventually I got through, and they dutifully sent me my free clear liquid remedy.

But disaster struck. Even though they were giving their remedy away for free, the government shut them down. Lest you doubt my story, a book on amazon.com, "The Cancell Controversy" by Louise B. Trull tells the whole story. Several years later Ed Sopcak , although less than fifty years old, died somewhat mysteriously. So it appeared that his discovery had died with him.

But not so. Researchers established that he had removed the memory from water and then imparted energies of love and healing to the water. Thus this positively energized water interrupted the negative energy patterns of disease, disabling it so that the body's own immune system could eradicate the disease. Say what? Water has memory? This is esoteric stuff. Never heard that before. And the knowledge died with Ed Sopcak.

But not so.

Ten years later a Japanese scientist by the name of Masaru Emoto made an amazing discovery. He flash froze water molecules. He then photographed each water molecule as it went from the liquid state to the solid state. He also experimented. He found that when he spoke to the freezing water molecule, it affected the shape of the molecule. If he said positive things, such as "I love you" to the water molecule, it transformed into a beautiful white crystalline shape, similar to that of a snowflake. If he spoke harshly, saying "I hate you", the water molecule shriveled and became dark. Dr. Emoto was rediscovering that water does hold memory and appears to have a consciousness. Weird stuff.

He wrote a book about his discovery, complete with pictures, and it became a New York Time's bestseller! "The Hidden Messages in Water", available on amazon.com, and became a worldwide sensation. There is also much information on the Internet about this structured water discovery.

So I now knew more about Ed Sopcak's discovery. But I did not know how to reprogram water to make it a healing agent. Years went by. Then I attended several summer conferences of the Tesla Society. Following the discoveries and inventions of Nikola Tesla, these yearly conferences are attended by hundreds of interesting "backyard" inventors and scientists. These guys really think outside the box! So I approached them for help. Within a few hours I had my answers. These wonderful minds freely exchange information, and they helped me immensely.

Now I know how to make structured water that heals and structured water that energizes. Now let's show you how to do this.

How to Make and Install a Healing Water Device on your home's water pipes:

What You Need

A. The demagnetizer strip

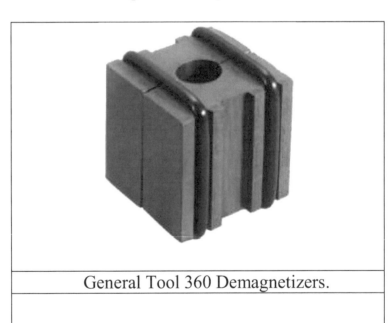

General Tool 360 Demagnetizers.

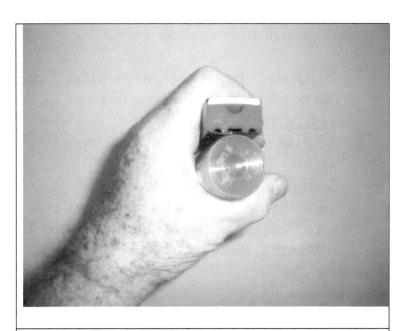

Schematic showing how 12 demag. strips are taped to the water pipe after being taped to a wooden strip that holds them together. The yellow tube represents the water pipe

Please note above (right) that 12 demagnetizer magnets are taped to a 12 inch paint stirrer stick as shown. The placement of the magnets on the stick, and the subsequent placement of the demagnetizer stick on the pipe must be correct. Keep the oval channel of the magnets away from the pipe.

You will need the following:

a. Six General Tool 360 Demagnetizers. You can buy them on the internet or go to http://www.generaltool.com.
b. A roll of regular black electrical tape (3/4 in wide).
c. A thin wooden strip, 1/8 to ¼ inch in thickness and 1 in by 12 inches. For this I get a free paint stirrer at the paint section of Walmart. It is the perfect size.

Do the following:

a. Strip the rubber bands from the magnetizers and separate the 12 separate magnet units.
b. Tape the units to the stick as shown. You will now have a demagnetizer strip that is 1 ft. long.
c. Tape or tie this unit to the water pipe in your home. Place it 3 ft. ahead of the energy card/plate.
d. Be sure to have the side of the demagnetizers with the large oval away from the pipe.
e. Note: Keep this demagnetizer strip at least 3 ft. away from your energy card at all times. Otherwise you may damage the energy card.

A. The energizer plate

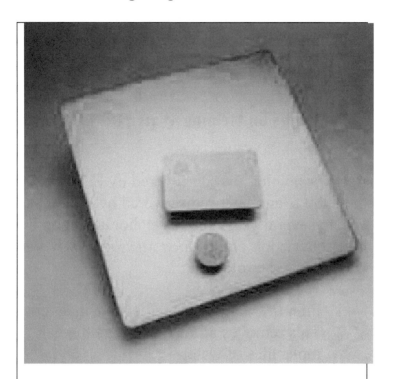

Use the small energy plate that is approximately
2 ¾ " by 4 ½" in size.

You can find a suitable energy plate at
http://www.energyplates.com/plates.html. Order
the "small" plate. They cost about $15.00.

Tape the plate on the water pipe 3 ft. downstream of the demagnetizer strip.

Comments on Healing Water Device Hookup

Basic principle: First discovered by Ed Sopcak in the 1980's, and later rediscovered by Dr. Masaru Emoto several years ago (as elaborated upon in his best-seller book *The Hidden Messages in Water*), we perform the following:

1. First the water is passed by a demagnetizer. This removes all memory from the molecules of water.
2. Then the demagnetized (dememorized) water is passed by an energizer, which places only positive vibrations into the water. The best healing energies are *Love and Gratitude*.

Points to watch out for:

1. Locate a section of water pipe entering the house. Usually this will be ¾ in. or ½ in. copper or PVC pipe.

2. Fasten the demagnetizer strip and the energizer plate onto the pipe, placing them at least three ft. apart. This is so the demagnetizer does not interfere with the energizer plate (which has positive energizers magnetically embedded in it). Be sure that the demagnetizer strip is placed first so that the water flows past the demagnetizer strip before it reaches the energizer plate.

3. You may use tape or plastic electrical ties to fasten the demagnetizer strip and the energizer plate/card to the pipe. I use black electrical tape.

4. Sometimes, because of the layout of the pipe in your house, you are not able to separate the demagnetizer strip and the plate by at least 3 ft... In this case, place them as far apart as is possible. Then wrap the energizer plate and the pipe to which it is attached with at least 4 layers of aluminum foil. This will help to shield the energy plate from any stray diamagnetic effects of the demagnetizer strip. In no case get the aluminum foil between the plate/card and the pipe to which it is attached because this would interfere with the energizer plate passing its positive vibrations to the water passing through the pipe.

5. If it is necessary to install the healing device under your kitchen sink, it may not be possible to keep the demagnetizer strip and the energizer plate 3 ft. apart. In this case, place the plate as close to the faucet as possible. Then wrap the energizer plate and the pipe to which it is attached with 4 layers of aluminum foil. This should adequately protect the plate from being demagnetized (ruined). Then install the demagnetizer strip as far from the plate as possible. It is best to attach the system to the cold water pipe.
6. As far as I know, this mechanism never wears out.

Final Comments:

The total cost of treating the everyday water that I drink is almost nothing. I fill old 1.5 liter wine bottles with water and place them in the sacred geometry 3-tubes, and process them for 3 days in my kitchen pantry. The only real cost is for the mailing tube sections that I use to make the cylinders that I keep in my kitchen pantry. They will last a lifetime.

The cost of making and installing a healing water device on my home water pipes was less than $100. It will also last a lifetime.

I love a bargain. These two systems for making structured water are bargains!

In addition, for approximately $300 you can find and install on your water pipes a system that imparts a Viktor Schauberger "spin" to your drinking water. Search the Internet for these devices.

I also order the herbal tea cancer remedy at http://www.remedies.net that is made with structured water. It is a great for strengthening the body. I get my immune system bolstered by the tea, and get their structured water as a bonus.

With these gadgets and features added to your inventory, you and your family are in for a delightful treat. Now just try to explain all this to your friends. Lots of luck!

The definitive book about Viktor Schauberger, on the NY Times Bestseller list for 2 years. Author is Callum Coats.

Viktor Schauberger

Interesting and provocative photo of a supposed flying saucer developed by Hitler's secret labs. Viktor Schauberger inventions were reportedly used. Some say this is why the US government kept Viktor imprisoned in a US laboratory in the desert until just before his death. Did he know too much?

Masaru Emoto

New York Times Bestseller for 2 Years!

Chapter Five
The David Hudson story

The Modern Discovery

In 1988 a wealthy Arizona cotton farmer by the name of David Hudson set out to analyze the soils on some of his cotton farms. He knew that the Spaniards had mined gold on these lands, and he sought to find out if there were any remaining precious metal deposits. So he sent samples of his soils in to laboratories for analysis. In the resulting chemical and spectrographic analysis, a substance was discovered that did not to seem to fit into the modern table of elements. After much further study, it was determined that they had stumbled upon a yet-as-unknown substance. Eventually he realized that he had rediscovered the material that had been known by the ancients for its ability to restore youthfulness and vitality.

David Hudson's full and amazing story is too long to fully repeat here. But if you choose to use a search engine to check out "David Hudson", or "Ormus" or "Ormes", or "white powder of gold" a whole new world of anti aging information will open up to you.

The David Hudson Story as he tells it:

[This is part of a transcript of a February 1995 introductory lecture and workshop by David Hudson in Dallas, Texas. It was transcribed from the video tapes which were recorded on February 10 and 11, 1995.]

[David Hudson speaks] "Basically this is the story of my quest for this material. I wanted to get an understanding of it, to be able to explain what it is. And my work began in this area for all the wrong reasons. I did not understand what I was doing. I didn't understand what the material was and it's only in the last four or five years that I've really come to an understanding, understanding truly of what the material really is. But basically the work began about 1975-76, and my primary interest for getting into this area is, was, like I say, for all the wrong reasons.

I am from Phoenix, Arizona. My father is the ex-commissioner of agriculture in the state of Arizona. My mother is the, was the state Republican's woman chairman. We're ultra-ultra right-wing conservative. Very, very ultra conservative people. All of my farming was done on a handshake basis. I even farmed 2,500 acres on a handshake with the Bureau of Indian Affairs and that's the federal government and no one farms with the federal government on a handshake and a verbal agreement but I did.

Our family is very, very conservative, very highly regarded in the community. All my vehicles have the keys in the vehicles right now. I'm here and they're there. Ah, we just... it's a very small community just outside of Phoenix where, you know, everyone knows everybody. Everybody knows the people going down the road. There just is no theft.

Anyway, when I became involved in this my thinking was to mine and process gold and silver to keep for myself. I was very disillusioned with the federal government's approach to our currency. They were devaluing the dollar, issuing this funny money, what they called Federal Reserve notes which I'm sure most of you people are aware of. They were not backed by gold and silver, and as you make more and more of these dollars they continue to devalue these dollars and you think you are making more money, but in fact all you are doing is moving into a higher tax bracket and paying more and more income tax.

And so you have less and less even though you are making more and more.

Anyway, I began buying gold and silver in the Phoenix area as bullion from refiners. Most of it was being refined from sterling silver scrap or electronic scrap. But, ah, a lot of the gold was coming from miners who were processing it by a process called "heap leach cyanide recovery". And they were heap leaching, um, these old tailings on these mining operations. I became very intrigued with this because we were very interested, in agriculture, in metal salts in our soils. I don't know, I think that here in Dallas it's much the same or further on west in the state, it's much the same as Arizona. We have a sodium problem in our soil. It's called "black alkali" and as the black alkali builds up in your soil you can put sulfuric acid on the soil and the sodium, which makes up the black alkali, becomes sodium sulfate, which is a white alkali. And then is water soluble and will leach out of your soil then. If you don't do this your soil is very oily and the water just won't penetrate and be retained by the soil and it's not very good for your crops.

And so we had been doing soils analysis and this concept of, of literally piling ore up on a piece of plastic and spraying it with a cyanide solution, which dissolves selectively the gold out of the ore. It trickles down through the ore until it hits the plastic and then runs out the plastic and into the settling pond. It's pumped up through activated charcoal where the gold adheres to the charcoal and then the solution is returned back to the stack. And the concept seemed pretty simple, and I decided, you know, a lot of farmers have airplanes, a lot of farmers have race horses, a lot of farmers have race cars... I decided I was going to have a gold mine. And, I had earth movers and water trucks and road graders and backhoes and caterpillars and these kinds of things on the farm and I had equipment operators, and so I decided I was going to set up one of these heap leach cyanide systems.

I traveled all over the state of Arizona, took about a year and a half, and I finally settled on a piece of property. And, ah, did some analysis and all and decided that this was the property that had the gold in it that I wanted to recover. I set up a heap leach cyanide system, began spraying the ore, and sure enough within a matter of a couple days, we hooked it up to the activated charcoal. And we analyzed the solution going in the charcoal. We analyzed the solution coming out of the charcoal and we were loading gold on the charcoal. And, you know, everything is just rosy. We're having a high old time. And I figured I could lose 50 percent per year mining gold and be as well off as buying the gold and paying taxes at 50 percent on the, on the profit with buying the gold. So, if other people had to mine gold and make a living, I could mine gold and lose 50 percent, and be as well off as making the money, paying income tax and buying gold with it. So I figured, hey, I ought to be able to do that.

So, what happened is, ah, we began recovering the gold and silver and we would take the charcoal down to our farm. We'd strip it with hot cyanide and sodium hydroxide. We'd run it through "electro winning cell". We'd get the gold out on the "electro winning cell". And then we would do what's called a "fire assay" where you run it through a crucible reduction. Now I am not going to elaborate on all this because I am not trying to teach anybody "fire assaying". I am just trying to explain the procedures here. This is the time honored procedure for recovering gold and silver and basically, it's, it's been performed for 250-300 years. It's the accepted standard in the industry.

 Ah, after we recovered this gold and silver for a couple of weeks, we began to recover something else. And the something else we were recovering as if it was gold and silver but it wasn't gold and silver. Our beads of gold and silver were actually getting to the point that you could hit them with a hammer and they would shatter. Now there's no alloy of gold and silver that will become that brittle. Gold and silver are both very soft metals and they don't alloy in any proportion that would cause them to become hard or brittle. Yet this became very hard and brittle. When we sent it to the standard laboratories for analysis, all they could detect was gold and silver with traces, and just traces, of copper. Something was recovering with the gold and silver. We couldn't explain. And eventually wet got so much of this in our recovery system that actually we were losing gold and silver when we recovered this other material. And so, you know, it wasn't supposed to be profitable, it's just supposed to be something that was interesting.

And so I said, "Shut the system down. You know, let's find out what the problem material really is". And chemically we were able to separate the "problem material" from the gold and silver and I had this sample of pure problem stuff, whatever it was. And you have to understand my background is cotton farming. I decided to go into agriculture but I hated chemistry, I hated physics, like most of you. And ah, I decided, well heck, you know if you just pay enough money to the right experts, you can hire enough PhD's, you'll be able to figure this problem out. So I went to Cornell University, where a man had written these papers on doing x-ray analysis and he took the sample of the problem material, which wouldn't dissolve in any acids or bases. It was cobalt blue in color. And he did an analysis on it and he told me it was iron silica and aluminum. I said it's not iron silica and aluminum. He said, "Well sorry that's what the analysis says it is". So, working within Cornell, we removed all of the iron, all the silica and all the aluminum from the sample. We still had over 98 percent of the sample. At this point he said,

"Dave, it analyzes to be nothing". (audience laughter)

He said, "Mr. Hudson, if you'll give us a $350,000 grant, we'll put graduate students to working on it". Well I had paid him about $12,000 thus far. He told me he could analyze anything down to parts per billion and now he's telling me I had pure nothing. He didn't offer to refund any of my money and so I said, "No thank you, I think for $350,000 I can get more information than you can". That was about 1981 and basically I embarked on a research program of my own.

I said to myself, "you know, I am going to fund the thing myself and I am going to get the answers to it". [End of David Hudson speaking]

The Adventure Continues:

So he did. David Hudson proceeded to spend years and several million more dollars researching the mysterious metallic substance that he had discovered. He even employed scientists and laboratories in England, Germany and Russia to assist him. Eventually it was discovered that his mystery element had hither-to-unknown physical properties. Eventually it was presented to Hudson that they had rediscovered an element that had been known by ancient civilizations. It had special spiritual and rejuvenating powers. At first, he named it "white powder of gold", later changing this to simply "ormus".

At this point, Hudson had spent eight million dollars of his own money. Now he was ready to build an actual plant to manufacture ormus. He needed an additional five million dollars to build the plant. He toured the country for three years and raised the money. He sold shares in the new plant.

He advised his investors that operations were ready to begin. Then disaster struck. At 2:00am one morning, a Federal force of 150 agents swept into the plant. They claimed that there was a dangerous gas leak. The plant was shut down, the plant was dismantled, loaded onto trucks and hauled away, the factory building was torn down, and the concrete foundation was bulldozed away and hauled off. Only bare earth was left.

Hudson was simultaneously hit with massive lawsuits by the government. He suffered a massive lawsuit. He sent out one last sad report to his investors. Then he dropped out of sight.

I know all about this because I was one of his investors. During the years that the plant was under construction, I had wondered if the government would allow knowledge of ormus to reach the public. Now I had my answer.

So this adventure, I thought to myself, is over. But I was wrong. Thanks to the wonder of the Internet, the information about David Hudson and his work survives.

The Internet to the rescue!

Six months later something very interesting happened. Formulas for making the white powder of gold and ormus began to appear on several Internet websites. The instructions on these websites even told you how to make it in your kitchen.

Since then, numerous groups around the country have formed to study this material. There are "Ormus Workshops" held at numerous locations. Experimentations have abounded. New, simple methods of making ormus have evolved.

David Hudson

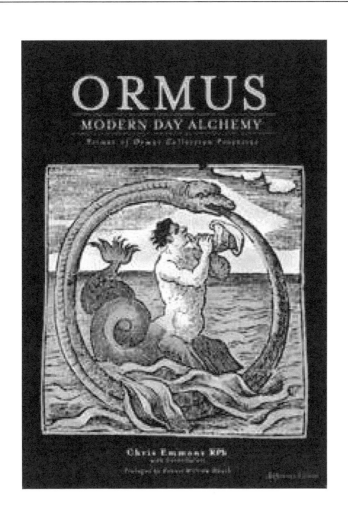

Book about David and Ormus by Chris Emmons

Wonderful books such as *"Lost Secrets of the Sacred Ark"* by the distinguished European historian and researcher Laurence Gardner have hit the marketplace. The Internet abounds with articles, study-groups, DVDs and books on the subject.

So the knowledge of ormus has not been lost this time. But as I am sure that you realize, most of the people in the world are not ready for this knowledge. It seems that the ancients knew to keep knowledge of ormus restricted to the privilege ruling and priest classes. Likewise they restricted the use of it to a few highly select individuals (the priests and ruling families).

For instance, in ancient Egypt, only the Pharaohs and the High Priests could partake of their ormus. It was known to them as shewbread. The ormus was baked into conical loaves of bread that were used in special ceremonies. There are hieroglyphs and wall engravings in Egypt that show the conical loaves of shewbread being presented to the Pharaoh or one of the Gods.

There is a mural picture of the Pharaoh presenting some shewbread to the God Anubis. This mural is at the Temple of Abydos.

Special Features of Ormus

As we progress into more detailed information about ormus, it is time to point out a few special things about ormus. As David Hudson continued to study his "orbitally rearranged molecules of rhodium and iridium that exist in the presence of gold", he and his researchers began to observe that this "ormus", whatever it was, had a consciousness. This was really weird. But, as researchers, they had the obligation to honor their observations.

Then they realized that their observations in this regard were totally consistent with ancient writing about this substance. It was the ancient Hebrew priests who would only let specially prepared priests into the presence of their stored ormus. And the ancient Hindu and Vedic texts also referred to the fact that only those who were properly spiritually prepared could prepare the elixir.

And it was the alchemists of the middle ages who always insisted that only the "pure of heart" and those with "purity of intent" who could make the philosopher's stone.

Suddenly all of this began to make sense. Because this mysterious element, whatever it was, had consciousness, it could sense the consciousness of the people about it. And apparently this mysterious substance, that we arbitrarily now refer to as "ormus", chooses to be around people of a higher quality of consciousness. This is very important when it comes to preparing ormus products. Simply put, the higher the quality of consciousness of the preparer, the greater the quantity, and the higher quality of the ormus that is produced.

So when you begin to take ormus, you want to be sure that a person who has a positive mind and is spiritually balanced has produced the ormus. It is also very important that the preparer "declare, or set, his intent to the ormus before he attempts to precipitate it into his product. In this regard, a properly balanced preparer will always say a prayer before beginning his preparation process, asking all of the angelic and nature forces to assist him in his endeavor.

Researchers also eventually discovered that there is ormus in everything. Some things have more ormus than others. For instance, grapes have an extraordinarily large amount of ormus in them. So does the brains of newborn babies. Water has ormus in it, especially water that carries minute amounts of gold and silver in it. Sea Water, heavily laden with minerals including gold and silver, is a treasure trove for the ormus producer.

Other features of ormus that are important to understand are that ormus is sensitive to bright light, electrical fields and magnetic fields. So I always try to keep my stored ormus away from bright lights. Likewise I do not store it near electrical appliances or electrical wires. The feature of ormus that it does not like magnetic fields is especially important to understand.

The Ormus Experience

When you are ready to try ormus, there are two ways that you can proceed. I shall discuss each of these ways.

1. Buy Ormus from a supplier on the Internet.
2. Make your own Ormus using the Wet Method.

Buying Ormus from a supplier on the Internet

Probably the best way for you to begin your adventure with ormus is for you to buy some ormus. The Internet is the way to do this.

Simply go to your favorite search engine and search the keywords "ormus", "ormes (another word for ormus), "white powder of gold", or "David Hudson". There are plenty of websites out there that deal with ormus. Probably the premium website is http://subtleenergies.com . This is the website of Barry Carter.

Barry Carter is a wonderful and pure man. He picked up the mantle after David Hudson went underground, and it is primarily due to Barry's unselfish work that the word of ormus has spread so far and wide. He has spent years touring the country, conducting workshops and talks about ormus. He presents internet forums about ormus. His website has grown to where it is the definitive source of information about ormus. Barry has never made a lot of money doing this. He just seems to do it because someone has to do it. Thank God for Barry Carter.

On his website Barry will recommend reliable sources of ormus. All of them are good and reliable. But my favorite is Don Nance. His website is http://oceanalchemy.com . I recommend that a beginner start with his "Great Salt Lake Manna". An 8 oz. bottle costs $50. This is a pretty much standard price. I started with this product. It is great for the beginner. Two weeks on this ormus and your world will begin to change right in front of your eyes. I recommend that you begin by taking ½ teaspoon of ormus twice daily, and gradually work up to a larger dose.

I also recommend Don Nance. Why? Because I know him personally, and I know that he has a pure heart and puts very pure intent into his products as he makes them. I also recommend him because he is one of the ormus pioneers who has unselfishly taught and guided many others such as myself as we struggled to learn the amazing truths about ormus.

I have also had a good experience buying "Four Realms Monatomic Gold capsules" that are available on amazon.com. Forty dollars buys a month's supply.

After you have begun taking ormus that you have purchased from a supplier on the Internet, you may then find that you are ready to tackle the challenge of making ormus yourself.

Chapter Six

Making Your Own Ormus!

The Wet Method of making Ormus

This method will make for you the same ormus that you previously bought from Don Nance.

This simple method can be done in your kitchen. It is called the wet method because it is made from sea water (or Great Lakes water), or a mixture of water and fresh sea salt. There are a number of recipes on the Internet that tell how to use this method to make an ormus product. I tried many of them, and I could never get them to work. Therefore for year after year I stuck with using ormus water made from my ormus magnetic trap.

Then I attended an ormus conference in 2009. One of the presenters was a wonderful man by the name of Don Nance. His talk to us was good, but what really blew me away was the generosity and lovingness with which he readily shared all of his knowledge with us. As I have previously mentioned, Don makes an ormus product that he sells on the Internet. Therefore one could assume that he would be reluctant to share his secrets with the world. Not so. He freely gave us wonderful and detailed instructions, as he personally demonstrated to us his wet method process. So now that is the process that I personally use. And that is the process that I am going to show you now.

You will need the following:

1. A large glass mixing bowl, at least 5 qt. capacity.
2. A hand-held ph meter. The one shown here costs about $40.00 and I bought it off the Internet. Be sure to get one

that reads from the 7.0 to 12.0 ph range.

3. Two wooden clothespins, glued together as shown, to hold the ph meter in the bowl. This frees up both of your hands for the mixing operation.

4. A pint (16 oz.) of concentrated and purified sea water or Great Lakes salt water. The bottle shown cost less than $10.00 and was found on the Internet. If you choose to try regular salt water, it will have to be carefully boiled and filtered to remove all impurities, and you will use 32 oz. of regular sea water.

5. A non-metallic stirrer. A regular kitchen plastic spoon works. I use a cheap wooden paint stirrer that is 12 inches long.

6. A glass measuring cup, at least one-cup capacity.
7. Pure lye (sodium hydroxide). I bought mine from a science supply company on the internet. The government has started making the Red Devil Lye Company put ingredients in their lye so it is no longer safe to use Red Devil Lye. Some people buy their lye from plumbing supply stores.
8. Two gallons of pure distilled water. I buy mine at the grocery store and pay about $1.00 per gallon. It is important to use pure distilled water because not only is it clean, it has no minerals in it that might interfere with the chemical reactions.
9. A small bottle of white distilled vinegar. This will be used in an emergency, should you accidently raise the ph of your mixture past 10.78. You will immediately add a small amount of the vinegar (an acid) to reduce the ph back down below 10.78. About 4 ft. of clear 3/8 inch plastic tubing.

10. reduce the ph back down below 10.78. About 4 ft. of clear 3/8 inch plastic tubing.

The Process

1. Add the 16 oz. bottle of sea mineral water to the bowl.
2. The distilled water should be a room temperature. Now add the distilled water to the bowl. Fill the mixing bowl to within 1.5 inches of the top with distilled water.
3. Put two teaspoons of powdered lye into the small glass measuring cup. Now add 16 teaspoons (the ratio is 8 times as much water *as there is lye) of water to the cup, and gently* shake to mix. Heat should be given off as the water and lye mix. Note: Never add lye to

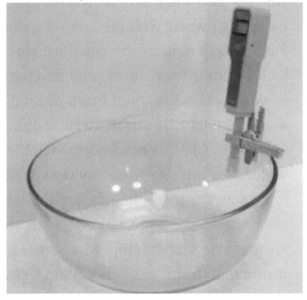

water, it may explode and burn your eyes or skin. Water and lye can be dangerous. It will burn your eyes, skin and clothing if you are not careful.

4. Turn the calibrated ph meter on and mount it in the wooden clothespin holder on the side of the bowl.

5. Check the ph of the water in the large mixing bowl. It should be somewhere between 7.5 and 9.0.

6. Now the most important and critical part. You must be very patient and methodical. If you try to rush this, you may ruin your batch. **Do this part very slowly.** Begin to stir the mixture of water with the mixing spoon. Now slowly pour a very small trickle of lye water from the measuring cup into the bowl as you continue stirring. From now on, you must continuously stir the water until the target ph of 10.7 is reached. Watch the ph meter carefully. As you very slowly add the lye water, the ph of the mixture should slowly rise. The emphasis is to pour **slowly!** Keep stirring the mixture at all times to insure that the ph meter is getting a correct

reading of the exact ph of the mixture. As you do this, you may observe the phenomenon that there are "level spots" in the ph reading. This means that you will get to a spot where, as you continue to add lye water, the ph does not go up. Be very carefully here. You have hit a level spot. The tendency here is to get impatient and add too much lye water. This will be a mistake, because once the level spot has been passed, the ph may just jump dramatically.

7. Your objective is to get the mixture raised to a ph of exactly 10.78. Many ph meters will read to only 10.7. This is good enough! Actually, when you get the mixture to a point where the ph meter fluctuates between 10.6 and 10.7 you are finished. This is good enough. You can stop now. What happens now is that the monatomic elements of gold, silver, rhodium, iridium and platinum settle out of the sea water when the ph gets to around 10.6 to 10.7

8. If you accidently get the ph of your mixture to 10.8 or above, quickly add a small amount

of white vinegar to bring the ph down again below 10.7, and start over.

9. Once you have your mixture at a steady ph of 10.6 to 10.7 you are finished. You will notice that a white material has begun to settle out of the water. This white material is the monatomic form of gold and other precious metals that is precipitated from the precious metals that naturally exist in the sea water.

10. At this point you must wait from 4 to 6 hours for the white material to finish precipitating. I usually wait overnight for this to happen. I place a large inverted platter over the mixing bowl to protect the ingredients, and then cover everything with a towel to keep light out.

11. The next morning you will notice that the white precipitate is now concentrated in the bottom 1/3 of the bowl. This wet white precipitate is what you want to harvest. So, using the 4 ft. piece of 3/8 inch plastic tubing, carefully siphon as much of the clear water out of the bowl as is possible without disturbing the white precipitate on the bottom. My procedure is to place one end of

the clear plastic tubing in the same wooden clothespin holder that I used to hold the ph meter. Then I adjust the end of the tubing so that it rests about 3/16 in. above the white precipitate. Then I place the other end of the tubing into a white plastic 5 gallon bucket that is on the floor. Suck on that end until the flow of water starts, then place that end into the bucket as the clear water drains out of the mixing bowl.

12. You will be left with the layer of white precipitate in water plus about 3/16 inch of clear water above it. This is the final product. Pour it into a pitcher and then store in glass bottles. I wrap my bottles in aluminum foil to protect the precipitate as much as possible from magnetic and electrical fields.

This is it. Now you have made a 4 to 6 week supply of ormus precipitate that is powerful and effective. Begin by taking ½ teaspoon twice daily and gradually build up to two tablespoons twice daily. The cost for this 4 to 6 week supply will be about $10.00. Not bad!

Further notes:

1. Many people choose to take their bowl that has the wet precipitate in it and add more distilled water to refill the bowl. They stir the mixture again. Then they repeat the settling process, again draining off the excess water. They may do this 3 or 4 times. This is called "washing" the precipitate. It removes most of the salty taste from the precipitate.

2. I prefer to not "wash" the precipitate. I have several reasons for this. First of all, I like the salty taste. And the natural sea salt is healthy for you, giving you beneficial minerals and trace elements from the sea water. But there is a more important reason. The salt in the mix protects the ormus particles from damage by light, electrical and magnetic fields. For some reason, the ormus likes to "hide out" in the salt matrix. So by leaving the salt in the mix, you have a better and stronger ormus product, with an improved shelf life.

Conclusion and Summary

Well, this has been a wild ride, hasn't it? Your belief systems have really taken a beating. It is really difficult for most people to accept what you have just read. I understand this myself, because I too had to go through this torturous tunnel when I first began this journey.

Congratulations to you for being courageous and brave. Yes, you are courageous and brave if you have made it to this point in the booklet!

This information could, of necessity, only be a brief overview of this very complex subject. Many questions may flood your head after you have read this material. I hope that you will use the wonderful abilities of the Internet and also the books listed in the Bibliography as starting points to do a more complete research of this fascinating discovery of ormus.

As I delved deeply into this subject, I gradually came to the realization that most people cannot handle this information because they are not, at this time in mankind's development, ready for this information.

Just as in ancient times, a small number of people are allowed access to this life altering information. But there is an important difference this time. In ancient times it was the high priest and the nobility who were entitled to partake of the white powder of gold. Now, in today's world, it is the brave adventurer, the seeker of truth, the most intelligent of people, who are allowed to access this knowledge. I like this. It certainly seems more fair!

So my best wishes to you as you begin your own exciting journey.

Additional Research Information

A Treatise: How Ormus repairs DNA and how it works

This information in this section is extracted from the book *The Philosopher Stone* by Henry Kroll.

In order for body cells to replicate they have to split the genes of the old cell to produce a new cell, the old cell sharing the genes with the new cell. The process of "unzipping" the gene codes completely, without damaging the gene codes, requires that certain minerals be present. These minerals are the monatomic mineral state of gold and platinum.

This critical process is made more difficult in these modern times because of our mineral-deficient diets. The soils that most of our vegetables and fruits are grown on have long-ago become deficient in most of the 84 minerals and trace elements that we need for perfect health. Linus Pauling, two-time Nobel Prize winner, stated,

"You can trace every sickness, every disease and every ailment to a mineral deficiency".

Each time a cell replicates, it loses a few of the gene chains called tellimires. When enough of the telomeres are gone, the cell dies. Thus it is the loss of these telomeres in the body cells that causes aging. If a cell has enough of the right superconducting minerals during cell replication it doesn't lose any telomeres. Therefore it can replicate indefinitely.

If a person's body is saturated with monatomic-state elements of gold and platinum, it is possible for a person to live for hundreds of years free of disease and without the problems of aging. [Perhaps this helps to explain the Old Testament people who were reported to live for many hundreds of years.]

In addition, the monatomic-state silver minerals in Ormus also play an important part in your health. The monatomic silver elements are tied to the very process of life itself. Monatomic silver kills disease organisms, promotes major growth of bone, and accelerates the healing of body tissue. It also speeds up the cell replication process.

Concerning the type of people who are able to accept ormus into their lives, Mr. Kroll states, "Some people are drawn into this knowledge from a very deep part of their soul". Enough said. If you are reading this, this probably means you.

Moses had several methods of making manna. When they were travelling in the desert, he and his brother Aaron took desert soil that was high in alkalinity and boiled it in alkaline water for several days. As the water boiled away, they added more alkaline water that they got from certain desert springs, making the brew even more alkaline. They then cooled the high-alkaline mixture and added vinegar to drop the ph. As the ph dropped, a milky substance formed. This was the monatomic states of the precious metals previously mentioned. The clear liquid was poured off, and the milky substance that was left over was their manna. This milky liquid was baked into whatever grains they had with them, and the resulting loaves were their "shewbread", their life-sustaining food that got them through the desert wilderness.

Anyone who has made Ormus using the Wet
Method will be impressed with the similarities
between these two methods.

Section B: Viktor Schauberger and his Energized Water:

The best way for us to proceed here is for you to
read the book "Living Energies" by Callum Coats
(available on amazon.com). The fascinating and
adventurous life of Viktor Schauberger is well
worth reading. And you should know about his
discoveries. When you pull the plug on your
bathtub, and the water makes a spiraling motion as
it exits through the drain, the water is forming this
spin in a natural motion to energize itself. It is the
same pattern that we see in tornadoes. Keep this
simple example in mind, for it explains much
about Schauberger's discoveries.

Many do, as I have, set up a device to spin the
water as it enters our homes through the water
pipes. I suggest that you may well choose to also

do this. The Internet will show devices that you can put on your water pipes to accomplish this.

Viktor Schauberger shows off one of his energy inventions.

However there is a severe limitation to this. The water does not store this energy. It is soon lost. Therefore it is not possible to "bottle" this energy for later use. Thus I am not going to spend much time on it.

However it is important to understand the principles taught by Viktor Schauberger.

Here is a special treat. This utube video shows devices using Schauberger technology and Emoto knowledge to create special water: http://www.youtube.com/watch?v=YVL6tfGhr8M

Section C: The development of Cancell water:

Note: This is a reprint of an article that appeared in Nexus Magazine January 1994:

Curing AIDS and Cancer
Interview with Ed Sopcak

<u>CanCell</u> is a carrier of vibrational frequencies which, despite being unapproved by the FDA, has cured AIDS, cancer, and other diseases.

Nexus Magazine, December--January 1994	Taken from vol 1, no 31 of Sovereign Scribe Magazine, PO Box 350, McKenna, WA 98558, USA. Phone 206 458 2699

ES: Ed Sopcak (pronounced 'Soap-check').

SS: *Sovereign Scribe.*

SS: How did you get first get involved in his type of work?

ES: I was working with free energy devices which is all about vibrational frequencies. During this time I had a friend named Don over at the University of Michigan who was at Saint Joseph's, who was a terminal cancer patient. They gave him six weeks to live. He got a hold of a product from Jim Sheridan called Entelev. He took that while at St Joseph's and ended up without any cancer in six weeks. That gets one's attention.

Now Jim Sheridan had started on the research project Entelev back in 1936. By 1947 he felt that he had a workable model that would cure about 38% of all cancer. He kept working. The more successful he got, the more unhappy the FDA got with him. So by the time 1984 came around he had had it; he quit and decided nobody wanted it and he just wasn't going to do it anymore. So this friend of mine asked me if I would make it for him. I said sure, get me the formulation and I would make it. So he did. Now Jim was looking at it from a chemical standpoint, having himself a degree in physical chemistry. I started looking at it from a standpoint of basic vibrational physics. So I made a few minor changes in the formulation based on vibrational physics. I made some and gave it to my friend. Then others heard about it who were terminal cancer patients and we gave it to them. This continued to grow. I've been at it for 10 years now.

All cancer is an anaerobic cell that has mutated. Cancer is a single disease. With the application of Entelev, Jim took an anaerobic cell and pushed it back through primitive, which meant it went back to the amino acids the body used to create the protein in the first place.

Now everybody recognizes that a cancer cell is an anaerobic cell. This is not news to anybody. The general attempt by people in cancer therapy is to take that weakened anaerobic cell and make it stronger with vitamins or whatever, and try to push it back to being an aerobic cell. You can't do that. Jim recognized this and his view was, rather than to make the cell healthy, he decided to just get rid of it. So he worked with the blockages within the enzyme system or the respiratory system and then he pushed the cell back through primitive and ended up with the amino acids that the body uses to create itself, and therefore the cancer no longer existed.

SS: Is this related to the hydrogen peroxide approach of creating an oxygen-rich environment whereby anaerobic cells can't function?

ES: Technically, but the first thing you must understand about hydrogen peroxide or these others is that nothing works chemically. Everything on the face of the Earth is electromagnetic vibrational frequency. Therefore, when you get into peroxide there's the assumption that since the formulation is H_2O_2, that it will always break to H_2O + oxygen and that is not true. It can also break into 2 OH radicals and very often does. But if it works for you, take it. If it doesn't, don't.

SS: So the vibrational changes brought about by CanCell, are these vibrations higher or lower?

ES: It starts out with a very high vibration and it degenerates over a 12-hour period. In doing that, as it comes down, it matches or gets into an interference pattern with viruses like the AIDS virus. It causes the virus to disassociate like the Memorex commercial with the glass when someone hits the note and the glass shatters. Well that's what happens with the virus.

SS: How does this relate with Rife's work?

ES: This is probably 50 to 75 years past the Rife technologies. We are now in a position on this planet where if anything plugs into a wall or uses a magnet to create the frequencies of the energy force, I would be suspect of it because the densities are too great We're working with high and extremely subtle frequencies. These frequencies cannot be measured with the technology we have today.

SS: So did you continue and advance the work of Jim Sheridan?

ES: I made CanCell for 6 months before I ever met Jim. We've been friends ever since meeting and I have a great deal of respect for him. We actually established a frequency that was a little above the frequency of oxygen. Not all oxygen has the same frequency. So what I believe that Jim was doing was starting out with a 6-ring organic compound and then he was manipulating the organic rings from 6 to 5 to 3 and various ratios. As you do this, every time you go from a 6- to a 5-ring compound, you increase the vibrational frequency. So he was really using chemicals to create a vibrational frequency in the water. So if you were able to take the dark material that Jim was making in the Entelev or early CanCell and you could filter out all of the dark materials, the material would still work. The chemistry had nothing to do with the function of the material. The only thing it had to do with was to create the frequency change.

So when we got to the point where the frequencies that I needed were higher than the frequencies I could get by the manipulation of chemicals, then we went to the new, improved CanCell several years ago. The new material analyses as pure water. The FDA told one of the doctors, so I hear, that they had run a clinical trial on CanCell. They found that it did everything I said it did. They figured there had to be something in the solution so they admitted that they tried using every known filter and couldn't filter anything out of it. Then they made a conscious decision that they would use the power of the US Government in order to prevent the American citizens from knowing anything as simple as pure water that had been programmed could cure many different illnesses. This is the condition it is in today.

SS: So how do you alter the frequency of the water?

ES: Well the frequency of water gets changed every time it rains or anytime you put it up against anything. In other words, water is a programmable crystal. If anyone doubts that, ask yourself where do snowflakes come from? A change in a physical state doesn't change the crystalline structure.

So the first thing you have to do, since water has been on this planet for 10.5 million years, you have to get the memory or the history of what the water molecule remembers out of there. You must deprogramme the crystal and get it as close to a blank as you can. Then you can reprogramme it with the frequencies that you want. You erase the memory with a distillation process. After the water is distilled and clean and the memory is taken out of it, then I just simply place another memory into it.

SS: The water will retain this new memory?

ES: Yes. It depends on what you do. You can get both stable and unstable memories in it. That's one of the catches. The other catch is to get something that will work as CanCell does as a vibrational catalyst, so that if you simply get it in the aura of the body it will function. You do not have to take it internally or let it wet the skin. All you have to do is put it on a cotton pad and close to pulse points on the body. If you do that you will pick up the frequency from the CanCell. It will align die frequency of the aura. This affects the frequency of the cell structure. Once you have a balance in the cell structure then the body will cure itself. Cancell doesn't cure anything. All CanCell does is to allow the body to put itself into harmonic and vibrational balance.

SS: So what exactly is the cause of cancer?

ES: That's easy. As I said it is a mutation of an anaerobic cell. So where does that anaerobic cell come from? There are basically two sources of them. One is if you eat any fat or oil that carries a lot of free radicals. The free radicals affect the nucleic acids and will reproduce themselves in a damaged state. Free radicals are in any partially hydrogenated things such as margarine, disco or all the oils on the shelves. Also most baked goods have partially hydrogenated oil in them. This is the basic cause of an anaerobic cell

Another thing is if you eat protein. Protein digestion is a two-stage process in the body. At the end of the first stage of digestion you will have a DNA chemical or frequency that will damage the nucleic acid, and unless you have an adequate supply of vitamin B6 within the system you don't complete the digestion of protein. Therefore you will damage those nucleic acids and you will have the production of cells in a damaged state. When they are damaged enough, when they are sitting in a voltage range of between a negative .17 volts and a negative .21 volts, and when you have in the system a bacteria that's classified as a progenitor crypto-cyden, then that will facilitate the change of an aerobic cell to an anaerobic cell. Once you have anaerobic cells in the body those cells will create energy. You do come up with ATP but it's in a different form or ratio. When the body recognizes that you're coming in with a different ratio, why then the function of the body is to circle the wagon to protect itself.

This is where all of the degenerative diseases occur, such as arthritis, lupus, diabetes, M.S., Alzheimer's, Parkinson's, etc. They will stay there and create all kinds of mischief. Now if, at the same time, some place along the line the body has a chronic demand for energy that is greater than the cell structure is programmed to deliver, the body answers that demand for energy by mutating the anaerobic cells. Since the mutation of an anaerobic cell is cancer, that's the cause. Usually the chronic demand for energy here is stress. Over the past 10 years I've spoken to over 40,000 people with cancer. Almost universally, at least 90% of the time you can say to a person diagnosed with cancer, "Within 6 months to 3 years ago, you went through a stressful situation. What was it?" They always then say, "Well how did you know that?" It is almost chiselled in stone that that is the case.

SS: This leads us to the approach taken by people like Dr. Bernie Seigal who say that cancer is related to one's attitude.

ES: He is correct. Now when I used to answer the phone about 4 hours a day, volunteers have since taken over this for me, but I could tell simply by talking to the person with a 95% degree of accuracy whether CanCell could be used successfully for them or not. A person who takes CanCell and has cancer and is still stay tag in a stressful situation, CanCell won't affect them at all. A person who is uptight and refuses to relinquish their stress, there's a problem there.

SS: Getting into a preventative approach, do free radical scavengers like vitamin E and SOD work?

ES: They sure do. Any of the antioxidants such as the B vitamins. Vitamin C, the water soluble one, and vitamin E, the oil soluble one, do work. The mineral is selenium. I don't personally take supplements of any type. I don't believe God put me here to be popping pills so I don't take things like that. But in general if you got your diet back to as much raw fruits and vegetables and nuts and minimally cooked foods, and if you did that and stayed away from animal products, I think you'd be a lot healthier.

SS: You mentioned previously a list of diseases caused by anaerobic cell reproduction. Do you have CanCell programmed to different frequencies for different diseases?

ES: No, I establish 34 energy clusters so it has a whole family of frequencies in it. See this is one of the problems with the FDA, because they think things happen chemically and all allopathic drags work vibrationally. Nothing works chemically.

See, you can go back to the later works of Einstein and he's telling the same thing I'm telling you in different words. He admits that there exists nothing in the universe except electromagnetic vibrational frequency. There is no such thing as mass. There is no particle in the nucleus of the atom. These things just simply don't exist. The only thing that exists is various forms of vibrational densities that appear to our perceptions as mass or solids.

SS: Is CanCell legal to use?

ES: It is not legal. Actually, it is legal but the US Government is using the full power of the government to prohibit people from exercising their first amendment right to freedom of speech or freedom of choice. They have unlawfully, without jurisdiction, prohibited me from giving this to people. Before the government felt they didn't want the competition from something that was effective, people would call me on the phone or write and inform me that they were diagnosed with terminal cancer. At that point I would send them CanCell with instructions and diet. If they followed the routine, about 8 out of 10 people ended up without cancer.

SS: How many people received CanCell?

ES: I've given away well over 30,000 treatments. Our files probably have about 10,000 testimonial letters, many complete with medical records. The dosage would be 1/2 cc under the tongue and 1/2 cc at a pulse point on the body.

SS: How much did it cost?

ES: I have never charged for it. I made a gift of this to everyone who needed help and I even paid for postage. There was no money involved and I sent back all donations.

SS: So if the FDA could conclude that CanCell was simply water, how could they block its use?

ES: In the hearing, Judge Bernard Friedman declared that water was a drug on the record.

Secondly, when the Kefauver Amendment FDA Act of 1938 came in in 1962, the 1962 amendment grandfathered all drugs that were in the marketplace prior to 1938, then CanCell should be grandfathered in. I filed a motion which he ignored. So I will resubmit that motion sometime this week.

Today, there is an unlawful injunction in place and they have prevented me from making a gift of this to anyone.

Back in 1990, the National Cancer Institute asked me for a sample of CanCell. We sent it to them. They tested it on 58 different tumour strains. It reduced or eliminated all 58. It was 100% effective. They put this in a report and signed it. They're sorry they signed it because now they are denying they ever did the study. They're trying their best not to let people know that there is something that would be helpful.

A little later, we were doing double-blind studies under World Health and FDA protocols on the AIDS virus in Africa. We were getting computer analyses of the data that we generated at the Texas Medical Center. They published an article in the *Explore!* magazine in July 1992. It said the people who were on CanCell with an additive to it had an increase in the CD4 count of their immune system of 604 points, and the placebo group had a decrease of 102 points. That upset them because that of course is the next great boondoggle in the world: how much money can we spend on AIDS research? So once they found out that you cannot get an increase of that magnitude in the CD4 count if the virus is still there, the conclusion was of course that CanCell is an effective treatment for AIDS. We know it is. We've done over 1000 double-blind studies in Africa and to this date the people who are doing the studies have refused to give me the studies of the report. The last reports, as I understand, were filed by the World Health Organization.

So they do know. The data is there. The US Government tested it and know it works and that is the reason they are so upset.

SS: So what's your next step?

ES: Well, we're fighting it. I would prefer to have the government follow the law. Once you get into law and this lawsuit that was brought against me, the first thing you have to understand is federal statutes. These federal statutes that you and I are subjected to apply only to corporate entities and to individuals who have signed a contract with the federal government. They admitted in open court that they do not have a contract with me and therefore, technically, they do not have jurisdiction over me or over CanCell. But they went ahead with the case.

The second point in this case is that they proceeded without a plaintiff. There was no harmed party. The FDA actually went out and tried to solicit a harmed party. They got names of people I sent CanCell to through the United Parcel Service, which was unlawful, but they did it. They went out and interviewed these people and none of them would sign or testify against me. Almost every one of them said that they would testify on my behalf.

So because there was no harmed party, there was never a hearing. I have the right to face my accuser. There wasn't an accuser. So Judge Friedman broke the law when he issued a permanent injunction prohibiting me from making a gift of CanCell to anyone. His law says that he must issue a temporary injunction to determine if it does irreparable harm. Obviously it doesn't. He issued a permanent injunction. When I put a motion in to set it aside on the basis that it was unlawful, he put in writing that since I was giving it away, of course it didn't do me any harm. The only people it harmed were those individuals who were benefiting from taking CanCell. So he admitted that. My reaction to all of this was that I continued to give CanCell because he did not enjoin me from making a gift of CanCell. The original injunction said he enjoined me from shipping a drug in interstate commerce. Of course commerce is what you do for a profit. So I kept giving it to people, but when I gave it to them I asked them to send a copy of their medical records to Judge Friedman, so he knew that he had erred by putting this injunction in place.

Friedman admitted in the show cause hearing that he had an extensive file that indicates that CanCell cures many different diseases and therefore it must be a drug.

When I appealed the original decision, they said I could not appeal it because I had to have a transcript before I could appeal it Since there was never a hearing there was no transcript. When I tried to point that out, Judge Friedman perjured himself on the record in writing over a 7-month period telling that there was a transcript, it was lost, it was in transit, it was misplaced etc. When I tried to appeal the entire case, the appeals court came back to me twice and said that they do not have jurisdiction over the case.

So it is at a standstill and it's obvious that it has to be a conspiracy since you have involved in this the FDA, the AMA and the American Cancer Society. You have Judge Friedman knowingly breaking the law and the appeals court knowingly has jurisdiction but says that they don't. When you get all of this together, it's obvious that there is a conspiracy to prevent the people from being able to use something that would benefit them.

I always thought that this was close to genocide. The International AIDS Foundation has filed a lawsuit in the international courts in Europe charging the US Government with bioethics violation, and it was accepted several weeks ago. This suit has to do with AZT, not CanCell. We'll see how that proceeds. If enough people scream, it will move. If not, they will bury it.

SS: How does CanCell work on AIDS?

ES: The same as the Memorex commercial on TV works. It hits the interference pattern that causes the virus to disassociate, to break up. It is quite effective. Our data indicates in 21 days it is 98% effective and that's actually reading the virus in the blood, not looking at CD4 counts. We actually put blood samples on a microscope, use a fluorescent dye and then read the virus in the blood. The original double-blind study had 101 people on CanCell and of that 101 people, 99 people were virus-free.

SS: Does CanCell work on all viruses and pathogens?

ES: Oh yes. Over in Africa instead of coming down with Kaposi's or something else, most of them came down with viral meningitis. The researchers in Africa tell me that CanCell knocks off viral meningitis in 4 days.

There is no such thing as an incurable disease any longer.

The only thing is that we just simply have not been able to apply or know what to apply to those diseases to get rid of them. CanCell is what I consider one of those advances in technology pointing to the point that nothing is incurable.

SS: So the body at optimum health has a certain frequency. If you have something that is going to help the body to eliminate various diseases with various characteristics, it must be helping the body to reestablish its own health frequency. So it matters not what the disease is; the body is out of tune with itself, and all you are doing with CanCell is reminding it of its natural frequency and the body gravitates toward it. Then anything in the way of that harmony would be dissipated.

ES: That's pretty good. Yes. You know, several years ago we had about 35 to 40 people in the Seattle area taking CanCell for AIDS and they were all responding. They were working through the University of Washington. Then all of a sudden something happened and it all folded within a couple of weeks. There are a lot of people in that area that had taken CanCell successfully for AIDS.

One of the problems I have with the younger generation who have AIDS and take CanCell: they gain weight and the T4 cells go up and back to normal, then 6 months later I get a call and they say they need another bottle—they got it again. I say, "You haven't learned anything and changed your lifestyle?" "Well no, why should I? The material is free and it's easy to get rid of so why should I change?" Whatever people are doing to expose themselves to the AIDS virus, don't do it!

Also, we do know that only 29% of those people who are exposed to the AIDS virus that become HIV-positive ever come down with AIDS. The immune system can control the virus and does control the virus in the majority of the cases. It's debatable once someone is exposed how long it is until they can show symptoms. They can remain normal and still be HIV-positive unless they get into a stressful situation or their health is damaged. That could dump their immune system, then they could become symptomatic.

We are spending $4.9 billion tax dollars researching AIDS. Of course you have to understand that the purpose of research is to accumulate knowledge, not to find a cure for AIDS.

SS: So the question is, how is CanCell made?

ES: About a year ago I was at the Texas Medical Center with a Dr Arthur Erikson. We were discussing the effects of CanCell on the AIDS virus. After about 3 days of meetings I got up and said to the group that CanCell is so far advanced beyond medical technology that there is not even a vocabulary in place that we can use to explain it to the medical scientists. Our first order of business is to develop a vocabulary.

So it's hard to tell people how you deprogramme and programme water. It does have memory. However, no mechanical device touches it, no electricity. It's all done differently. If you had the vibrational frequency of the 60-cycle current, that would destroy it. If you used magnets or any metallic device, that also has a vibrational frequency and those frequencies would tend to override.

SS: Could you give us a hint? Is it done through human consciousness?

ES: Only partly. That does have an effect upon it. The human mind can destroy it. Not only mine but anyone else's. This IS part of positive thinking. I don't know how spiritually inclined you are, but one of my observations goes like this: it is the intent that the individual who is creating the material, their mental intent has an effect upon the product. The reason conventional or allopathic medicine doesn't work and never will work is because those individuals that are creating it are creating it not to cure anybody, but their main intent is to make a profit. It does make the profit but it is not effective as a cure. So you would have to change the entire effort of the medical profession and the pharmaceutical industry before you could get allopathic medicines to work again. I don't care what Clinton does or anyone else, unless they make some basic change there, nothing they do is going to work, unfortunately.

If you read a couple of hundred books on the art of positive thinking and that type of subject material, well then you will start to change the direction that you are thinking and you'll be right where you should be. Try not to be too scientific about it. Every time someone does they get it all screwed up.

This material is advanced to the point where you have to go back and start with Einstein and realize that he in his later writings indicated that nothing exists in the universe except electromagnetic vibrational frequency. There is no such thing as mass. Once you understand that and that everything is electrovibrational magnetic energy, then everything else becomes quite plain. Again, what we consider mass or solids are simply vibrational densities. If you can agree with that, then the rest of all of this becomes easy, because all you're doing is providing a vibrational catalyst that allows the body to tune itself or become in vibrational balance. When it does that it eliminates all vibrational density in the body. When it eliminates the vibrational density which we call disease, the disease no longer exists. That's purely and simply all it is.

SS: So couldn't a person who is clear in their attitude and consciousness infuse those vibrations into a substance which could carry that vibration?

ES: Yes, you can do that. But at the same time, if you can do that you could cure any illness you had. The mind is powerful enough to do that. This is what they call the placebo effect. The placebo effect actually runs close to 30% in many cases.

SS: So CanCell is more that just someone holding up a bottle of water and thinking into it.

ES: Oh absolutely. Yes.

SS: It's a whole new non-technical field of technology.

How Our Healing Water Works

About 20 years ago scientists discovered that water molecules could store memory. Dr. Masaru Emoto achieved fame with his New York Time's bestseller book "The Hidden Messages In Water." He showed that the molecular structure of water changed with the type of memory placed into the water, and he developed methods of photography to show molecules of water after being imprinted with various types of positive and negative messages. IBM scientists, as we speak, are researching ways to harness the memory storage ability of water molecules in order to develop better computer memory storage capacity.

All water carries the memories and information that have been implanted into it. Some of our water has been around for thousands of years. Therefore it carries memory imprints of its experiences during these thousands of years. Some of these memories were positive (the joy of a childbirth, for example) and some of these memories were negative (the massacre of an Indian village, for example).

Your body is 80 to 90 percent water. You know this. What you did not realize is that the water in the cells of your body still carries all of its previous memory, some of which is positive, some of which is negative. That is okay, as your body is used to dealing with this situation.

About 15 years ago a researcher named Ed Sopcak interviewed approximately 100 people who had cancer. Without exception, he found that all of these people had suffered a severe negative experience from six months to twenty-four months prior to the onset of their cancer. Examples of these negative experiences were divorce, termination of employment, betrayal by a spouse or friend, or loss of a child or loved one. Based on this interesting information, Mr. Sopcak developed the postulation that the cancer cell was based on a negative frequency vibration. He experimented. He was an electrical engineer, so he used an electrical approach to solving his problem. He was quite successful, and for a number of years he cured thousands of cases of cancer. Here is how he did it:

1. He used principles of electrical engineering to remove all previous memory from some water.
2. He then subjected the water to only positive memories (mostly the vibrations of love and harmony).
3. Then he fed this only-positive vibration water to his people who had cancer. Their cancer went away.
4. Mr. Sopcak explains what happens as follows: "When the water that has only positive vibrations in it is taken into the body, it is foreign to all of the water in your body that is comprised of both positive and negative vibrations. It is especially foreign to the cancer cells that are made up of only negative vibrations. These cancer molecules,

made up of only negative vibrations, are thrown into disarray by the arrival on the scene of molecules of water that are all positive. This disrupts the frequency patterns of the negative-only cancer cells, allowing your body's natural defense and immune system to remove them and expel them from the body."

5. Mr. Sopcak then later discovered that these same healing principles applied to many other of the body's illness and diseases.

In approximately 1990 Ed Sopcak appeared on the nationwide Maury Popich television show, explaining his method and introducing many people who had been cured of their cancer using his water. He named his water Cancell. Unfortunately Mr. Sopcak dies shortly thereafter, and his healing system has never been further developed.

In 2002 Dr. Masaru Emoto basically rediscovered this healing modality. He uses a different method to remove the memory from the water (he uses distillation) and then instills the water with only loving positive memories. He has named his healing water "Hado Water". His method is explained in his books, which are available on amazon.com.

How Mike makes his Superwater

Here is the system that I have installed in my home. It may give you some ideas for a system for your home or office.

1. The water for my home enters through a main ¾" water pipe. Along this pipe I have taped a demagnetizer magnetic strip. As the water passes these magnets it is demagnetized and all memory is removed from the water.
2. Three feet downstream from the magnetic strip I have taped an energizer plate. This energy plate imparts the energies of love and harmony into the water. Now the water has only positive energies in it.
3. The water then passes through a Viktor Schauberger energizer that is installed in the pipe. This device implants a spin to the water that energizes the water.
4. I fill a water bottle at the faucet with this water. I then place the bottle in a 3 concentric cylinder device for 3 days. This

imbues the water with universal harmonic energy from the universe.

5. My Superwater is now ready to drink. I may also add a small amount of ormus water to further enrich my water tonic.

This system is not expensive to install, and it never wears out. If all of this information is of interest, I strongly suggest that you obtain some of the books that I recommend, and read further. Of course, the Internet is also a wonderful research tool, and can assist you greatly.

A Story

Now I wish to tell you a story. Back about 1900 scientists invented penicillin as a new medicine to fight infection. In those days infection was a big killer.

Penicillin, and its amazing infection fighting abilities, was duly reported in all of the major medical journals, and was widely publicized. But it was ignored by the establishment. The general consensus was that it could not possibly do what it was reportedly doing. So it just got ignored. For almost fifty years it was ignored.

Then World War II came along. The many medical emergencies that occurred forced the medical establishment to try penicillin. It became an immediate success and our lives were changed as a result.

So why do I tell you this story? I believe that the information contained in this small book is similar to the situation about penicillin. Society's ability to process and accept this information is just not there yet.

But this does not mean that you and your family and friends cannot benefit from this knowledge. The decision is yours!

Bibliography for further research:

Note: I have listed the books in the order of importance that I found them to be in writing this booklet.

Pyramid Power by Max Toth and Greg Nielsen; Warner Books Inc., ISBN: not shown

Serpent in the Sky; The High Wisdom of Ancient Egypt by John Anthony West; Quest Books, ISBN: 0-

8356-0691-0

Egyptian Harmony, The Visual Music by
Moustafa Gadalla; Tehuti Research Foundation,
http://egypt-tehuti.org, ISBN 09652509

The Return of Sacred Architecture by Herbert
Bangs; Inner Traditions (Bear and Company), ISBN:
1-59477-132-4

Sacred Geometry, Philosophy and Practice by Robert
Lawlor; Thames and Hudson, ISBN 0-500-81030-3

Secret Teachings of all Ages by Manly P. Hall,
H.S.Crocker Company, Inc. ISBN 978-0-9753-0934-6

Architecture for the Poor by Hassan Fathy; University of
Chicago Press, ISBN 0-226-23916-0

The following interview appears on the website https://sandiegoyuyu.com/

YuYu interview Masaru Emoto

2007年04月30日最終更新日:2020年10月12日

Masaru Emoto

N.Y. Times Best Selling Author

It's like the chicken and the egg, which came first? If you have good water then of course it will have beneficial results for your body, soul and self. By the same token if we constantly ingest poor water it will have the opposite effect.

—— **What was it that got you interested in water?**

Well, it wasn't until I was in my forties that I even became interested. Before that I had no interest in religion, philosophy, or science...I didn't believe in a God. I was just working in my trading business when a colleague introduced me to colloidal water that helped me heal this terrible foot pain that I had been having. That experience was what sparked my interest and further investigation. Then as I started to study the Hado water I began to understand that the reason for my interest were the memories I had from past lives.

—— **Where did you spend your past lives?**

Many different places; in Mexico as an Incan, a Mayan, in Ecuador and many other areas, including lives in North America. That is why when I travel to any of those places I immediately feel very comfortable…like I belong there, because of my past life experiences. I feel a deep connection. The psychic who did my past-life readings told me that I've had hundreds of past lives and in my previous lives I had always attained the level of a master—each connected with water in some way. Things didn't usually work out for me though because of my arrogance and self-aggrandizement, things ended in disaster. This time I have been reborn as a typical "ojiisan" (old man) to try and learn from my past- life mistakes. As a very typical person I now know that by myself I cannot hope to do everything. That is why I have all of these helpers to work with me in all of this.

—— Can you heal people with hado water?

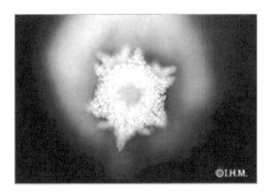

Water after being exposed to the word Peace.

Yes. As a healer I've used my power and knowledge of hado water to heal more than 10,000 people. I've healed them from such things as AIDS, cancer and various other serious diseases just through water. I used to heal with the help of a magnetic resonance analyzer (MRA) and through this machine I can measure Hado. Through the MRA I can connect with people and can get a reading on internal information to find out what is happening with their bodies and measure the results. Before, directly contacting patients in

Japan legally wasn't allowed, so I had patients hold the device bar and I observed the MRA readings and I'd ask questions and get the feed back from the machine. It was very successful, but now that I look back it was a pretty scary experience.

—— **What was it that scared you?**

It's because I could feel the bad vibrations from patients. Sometime I would absorb really bad vibrations from them—all that bad energy—was very dangerous to be around. I not only had to take in the bad energy, but I had to concentrate on releasing it. Once I was distracted by a beautiful women and the bad hado energy coursed through me and jolted my body, so I really need to actively focus on ridding my body of that bad energy. So the poison from the of 10,000 people's problems, at the DNA level, chemical level, past-life, karma, disease and psychological troubles, have passed through me. I'm surprised that I'm still alive, because so many of the people who were doing this are dead. It's because of love and gratitude that I'm sitting here talking to you today. Back then I was still smoking like crazy because of all the stress…I needed it as a release for the pressure, but now I don't need to.

—— Do you still personally heal people anymore?

I don't do any healing anymore...its takes a lot of energy from me and now I'm getting too old for that. There are many problems all over the world and you fix one thing and another thing comes up. So through my travels, lectures and books I am spreading the word to let people heal themselves physically and mentally. By myself it is impossible, but through my books and lectures I can reach even more people. To carry on my work I have already trained a number of hado practitioners to use the MRA in Japan and have started the Hado Instructor School in Los Angeles.

—— What led you to begin your experiments in photographing water crystals?

These healing experiences are what lead me to study, explore and develop the crystal philosophy. We've found that healing happened just by drinking this hado water with the beautiful crystals formations. As I studied and worked with water I began to realize that water was affected by the information or vibration that it took in and was exposed to. I had this theory that we could change the structure and improve the quality of our water by exposing it to positive thoughts, images and sound, but I had no way of physically proving it. One day, I was reading about how there are no two snowflakes alike and the idea came to me that we could freeze water and then photograph the results. So I immediately had one of my staff members, Mr. Ishibashi, begin experimenting with taking photographs of the water. For months he worked on this with no success, only disappointment. In fact, he was almost certain that it couldn't be done, but I kept reassuring him, telling him how confident I was that he'd find a way. Little by little my passion and confidence rubbed off on him and he too started to believe that we could in fact do it. At the same time we were gradually improving our methods in conducting the experiments. Finally, in 1994, we broke through. First, we put water in a bottle and expose it to a word, picture or some music, and then we'd put samples of the water in Petri dishes and then freeze the samples. After a few hours the water would freeze and then we would light the sample, then we'd observe crystals forming as the temperature rose and the ice started to melt. It takes a minute or two and then, like a flower blossoming, you can see the crystal formation taking place and spreading.

—— **So is this the message the water holds for us?**

In my two books, I discuss aspects of this; "The Hidden Message of Water" tells of my philosophy that I learned from the water, the message of love and gratitude, while in "The True Power of Water" I explore what led to my developing this philosophy and that we are the water and the water is us. Those are the messages that we can learn from water. Throughout my childhood and beyond, I had this terrible reoccurring nightmare, for 50 years, usually once a week: I was living in Yokohama, up on a hill, with a view of the Tokyo Bay. Looking out I hear a strange sucking noise and then the next thing I see is the ocean splitting in two! The water parted just like in a movie, revealing the bottom and then in a moment a huge tsunami comes roaring towards me. I gasp and run away and just as I'm being overtaken by the giant crushing wave I wake up in a sweat. Every time it's the same … every time for 50 years. I really didn't know why, but for the last six years 6 years since I published my first book I haven't had the nightmare anymore! We self-published the book and through word of mouth its popularity grew. Now it is published all over the world, in many different languages, and was on the NY Times best sellers list for 17 weeks. I am only the 2nd Japanese author to accomplish that, the other being Sony's Mr. Morita.

—— What effect does good water have on our bodies?

It's like the chicken and the egg, which came first? If you have good water then of course it will have beneficial results for your body, soul and self. By the same token if we constantly ingest poor water it will have the opposite effect.

—— Since our bodies and this planet are composed primarily of water, can we change the world if we think differently about water?

It's the same idea on a different scale. Just now the world is terribly sick and if it continues to get worse, even if we do change the quality of the water, the world will still be in big trouble. The world needs to heal. It is almost impossible to change the whole world, but we can change people and make them better. First, we need to focus on things in our own lives and neighborhoods, then, if enough people change, we can make bigger changes as we move from individuals to neighborhoods and our cities and so on. In this way it won't be impossible.

—— **You mentioned that we should start small, start with ourselves in order to create change. What do you do in your daily life with water?**

During breakfast lunch and dinner, everyday I drink water and take care of myself and also pray. The first thing I do everyday is to verbally express my love and gratitude towards the water and I do the same each night. After work I sometimes feel like drinking, which good because the intrinsic hado of alcohol is good if done in moderation and in positive settings and topics.

—— **As you show in your slides the source of the water makes a difference. What kind of water do you suggest drinking?**

Basically, you should drink water from your area;

where you are living. That is because our body is constructed of the minerals taken from the water where we were born and are living. The resonance and the purity of the water is crucial because the water where you were born is the essence of your being. To drink the water from where you were born will resonate more greatly with you, more than other water.

—— **Do you think we are currently on the right path as a civilization and planet?**

Our world is going down the same path as we have previously when we lost civilizations. There once existed other continents on our planet, Mu, that had Hawaii at it's center, Atlantis and Lemuria. If we keep following the same path we are on we will meet the same fate as Lemuria, Atlantis and Mu—catastrophe! The temperatures around the world are rising an average of 3.6 degrees Farenheit and if we keep on at this pace it will climb to 5.4 degrees F. If a human body temperature were to rise by 3.6 degrees he or she would be considered sick—the earth is the same. If the earth's temperature keeps increasing, as it is predicted to do, what will happen? If the earth were a person it would die. But the earth won't die; the earth will start getting rid of the causes of the rising temperatures. There will be earthquakes, flooding, hurricanes…all trying to get rid of the reason, which has been the enormous increase in the population. If the population trend continues and we don't change we won't be able to survive on earth anymore. The fossil fuel we increasingly use for energy is causing our planets temperature to rise and if we keep using it the temperatures will continue to increase. So the time has come for us to stop using energy from fire and develop and use energy from water! The fire era is also known as man's world, however, the 21st century is the Age of Aquarius and is the era of women.

——— **Most of us realize the importance of clean water and how vital it is to us, is there something we are missing?**

Water Crystals formed reflecting "Love and Gratitude" and"arigatou"

There are many mysteries within water and most people don't really know what the water is and that is why they really don't know themselves. If you know water you'll get to know about yourself. When we were fertile eggs we are 90% water, as a baby that becomes 80%, and as adults we are made up of around 70% water. As we age we lose water and when our water percentage drops below 50% we die. Water is the only source that carries the source of vibration, or Hado, and through my studies I've discovered that the water crystals are really the manifestation of vibration. When we raise that vibration through positive thought or music we revive the water in us and revive ourselves and we feel happier or stronger. I've been looking at the vibration and now I know what the vibration is.

—— The water crystal pictures are so beautiful, what are some of the experiments you did?

As we were documenting the water crystal

formations from various parts of Japan and throughout the world we realized that the quality of the water crystals depended on more than just whether the water was natural, tap or bottled— perhaps water can be affected by hado, or subtle information or vibration, both good and bad. To test this we exposed the water to different sources of information. In our first test of this we placed labels on two identical bottles of water. One said, "thank you," and formed beautiful water crystals, and the other said, "you fool" and produced only fragments of crystals. After discovering water's ability to change and its sensitivity to external sources of information we began exposing it to other sources, music, prayer, pictures and so on.

—— **What were the results?**

Time after time water responded to positive information by forming beautiful crystal formations, regardless of the language—it responded to the essence of the information! This can be from across the room or across the ocean. The most dramatic and beautiful by far has been the reaction to "love and gratitude". It enhances the immunity of the water, the clarity. Through the power of prayer, love and gratitude, I have

118

witnessed water in reservoirs healed through the work of Buddhist Priests. Not just love and not just gratitude, but together. Love is the active and gratitude is the passive. Only when there is the act of receiving can there be a giving. So I'm giving out active energy right now and you are a receiver. Once you start vibrating, it turns into an active energy and from now on you have to be active to pass on this energy to others. This is the basis of free energy, that God created. God, the creator, made the earth and left it to us and for us to create. God created water. God gave love and gratitude to the water; the secret of H20 is the ratio of 1:2, which is 1 (love): 2 (gratitude). On our face we have 2 ears and one mouth. What would you do if you had 2 mouths, you might have a fight and that would only lead to destructive energy.

That's why I love doing this kind of interview because the questions make me think about answers that I didn't realize before and so it is a chance to see another part of me that I was unaware of. It's a chance for self- discovery. When you deal with people their actions and reactions are all different, but the idea of love and gratitude is the same. Even when we are talking right now I can feel the vibrations and want to send out positive vibrations.

—— Me too! It is that interaction that makes life exciting.

That's why I love doing this kind of interview because the questions make me think about answers that I didn't realize before and so it is a chance to see another part of me that I was unaware. It's a chance for self-discovery. When you deal with people their actions and reactions are all different, but the idea of love and gratitude is the same. Even when we are talking right now I can feel the vibrations and want to send out positive vibrations.

—— Your lectures talk about resonance, how do you feel that now that your message is resonating with so many people through your books and movies?

It makes me really happy and so I can't quit now. Since many are resonating with me now, they receive my energy and as we resonate together this create new vibrations, which come back to me many times over.

(09-01-2005 issue, Interviewed by Terry Nicholas)

Masaru Emoto ----------------------

Masaru Emoto is an internationally renowned Japanese researcher who has gained worldwide acclaim. He is a graduate of the Yokohama Municipal University's Department of Humanities and Sciences with a focus on International Relations. In 1992, he received his certification from the Open University as a Doctor of Alternative Medicine. He is an author, lecturer and healer. He has written and self-published numerous books on water including the N.Y. Times best selling"The Hidden Messages in Water"and others including his latest The True Power of Water. Through high-speed photography Masaru Emoto has shown the consequences of thoughts and other vibrations on the formation of water crystals. He is the head of IHM Research Institute, President of IHM CO LTd. And Chairman of the International Hado Fellowship. If you want to learn more visit www.hado.net

----

Viktor Schauberger: The Man Who Taught Us Water Is Alive

https://www.nspirement.com/2019/02/22/

Before Dr. Masuru Emoto proposed that human consciousness has an effect on the molecular structure of water, Austrian naturalist Viktor Schauberger (1885-1958) said something far more fascinating. He theorized that water is alive.

Living water

"Were water actually what hydrologists deem it to be — a chemically inert substance — then a long time ago there would already have been no water and no life on this Earth. I regard water as the blood of the Earth. Its internal process, while not identical to that of our blood, is nonetheless very similar. It is this process that gives water its movement," Schauberger once stated (*Whole Life Times*).

As a young man, Schauberger would sit by a rushing stream and observe its movements with great interest. It was these observations that eventually convinced him that the mechanical view of water was false. He realized that water, like any other living organism, has memory and responds to its surroundings.

Schauberger made this clear when he explained water's natural ability to move upwards in a healthy forest ecosystem. He made this conclusion after studying a stone-covered spring with a roof overhead. When Schauberger took away the stones and the spring got exposed to sunlight, the spring water slowly disappeared. However, when he put back the stones, the spring water magically reappeared. It was as if the water had a memory of the stones and responded to their presence by "seeking" them out through an upward movement from deep beneath the earth.

When he put back the stones, the spring water magically reappeared. (Image: via pixabay / CC0 1.0)

Through his research of water streams, Schauberger posited that water twisted and pulsated in very specific ways when it was "healthy." This allows it to maintain purity and function as an energy channel, while also transporting waste and nutrients for all organisms. He was of the opinion that Earth's water ecosystems have been deteriorating since World War I and warned that humankind will eventually bring itself to the brink of collapse due to our inability to understand how all life on Earth is interconnected and interdependent.

"Schauberger's vision is entirely holistic, a term and a worldview that is often misunderstood within the mainstream of our culture. His vision was of life as a great drama, with all organisms playing a part. Every cell and water molecule sounds a note that collectively become the music of life, sometimes discordant, but generally developing a harmonious and increasingly complex orchestral creation. We may have to go through a level of breakdown in our culture before we can really appreciate Viktor's extraordinary prescience and guidance," according to Schauberger.co.uk.

Often mocked for his theory that water is an actual living organism, various scientific studies over the past few years are now lending credence to Schauberger's ideas.

Experimenting on water's consciousness

Scientists from the Aerospace Institute of the University of Stuttgart in Germany conducted a study in which a group of students was asked to collect a single droplet from the same body of water. When researchers observed the collected droplets, they were stunned.

They discovered that the microscopic pattern of the droplets varied from each other drastically depending on the student who collected it. The droplet seemed to be responding to the person, thereby creating unique microscopic patterns for each individual.

The team decided to conduct a second test in which they put a flower in a body of water. When they examined the droplets collected from the water, they found that every droplet produced the same pattern. But when they placed a different species of flower in the water, the droplets collected showed a completely different pattern. The scientists concluded that water has memory.

When they placed a different species of flower in the water, the droplets collected showed a completely different pattern. (Image: via pixabay / CC0 1.0)

When one compares these results to the fact that 70 percent of the human body is literally composed of water, exciting new possibilities emerge. Given that water has the ability to store information, it is possible that every drop of water in our body is potentially a storehouse of memories. Even the tears we shed might contain information about the sad memories that triggered them.

An Interview with Jim Sheridan's son

(Jim and Ed Sopcak were partners)

As found on
https://strongholdofhope.com/tribute-james-sheridan.html

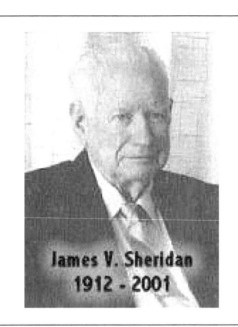

Jim Sheridan

Tribute to James Sheridan

James Sheridan and "The Project"
by Marge Sheridan Dubuque

On April 11, 1912, my Dad, James Sheridan was born in Hazelton, Pennsylvania to a coal miner and his wife. He was the second of three sons. As Dad grew it became obvious to his parents and teachers that he had some very special gifts, including an incredible aptitude for math and science. He excelled in school, played the trumpet in his high school marching band, and enjoyed camping and hiking in the mountains with his father. He also worked while he was in high school; 15 hours a week in a clothing store and later 54 hours per week as an elevator operator.

Dad's parents could not afford college and he might have ended up in the mines but for the money he had saved, the intervention of his high school principal and assistance from a state senatorial scholarship. He was admitted to Carnegie Tech (now Carnegie Melon University) in Pittsburgh, PA. He planned to become a mining engineer, but during his freshman year all thoughts of this disappeared as it became apparent to him that he was destined to be a chemist.

During his early years and throughout his lifetime, Dad had an abiding faith in God. He was often frustrated with organized religion because as he put it, "They wouldn't let ME talk to God." Dad believed that God communicated directly with His followers if they would just listen and he believed in miracles as God's answer to everyday prayer. This belief played a major part in the formulation of his goals. In his teens, Dad spent a great deal of time thinking about the course his life should take, and in the end, decided to ask God for the knowledge that would help him find a cure for cancer. The switch to chemistry came when Dad began to have a recurring dream in which he saw a chemical formula. He did not understand the formula and could not find anyone to explain it to him. Several events and another dream would send Dad down the path that he followed until his health failed him in his 80's.

The first event occurred in April of 1931 during Dad's sophomore year at Carnegie Tech. The college was having an open house for high school students. Dad was working on an experiment, which resulted in a beaker of yellow liquid being left on his desk. Two students asked, "Is that chromate in that beaker?" Dad said, "Yes." The students asked how to get it out and Dad told them all you had to do was add an acid. Dad thought any acid would do and selected one at random and poured it into the beaker. Much to everyone's <u>surprise</u> and delight the solution separated into bands of color as in a rainbow: red, orange, yellow, green, blue, and violet. Others tried the experiment and got the same result; however, only the acid picked at random produced the colorful display.

The second event was Dad taking a special course called "Theory and Thermodynamics of Solutions." This incident became a favorite family story over the years. As a joke, Dad pointed his finger at his professor Dr. Jake Warner (later president of Carnegie Tech) and said, "What is the DeBye Theory?" Jake responded, "You are not ready for that yet." After the summer break, Dad chanced to meet Jake who pointed his finger at him and asked, "What is the DeBye Theory?" Dad replied, "You said I was not ready for that yet." To which Jake said angrily, "Young man when you ask a question you are ready for the answer. I want you to take my Thermodynamics class." Dad explained that he had not had the two years of physics required, but Jake said he did not care and Dad took the course. The following year, Jake said to Dad, "Why aren't you in my thermodynamics class?" Dad said he had already taken it. Jake did not care, so Dad took the class for the second time. The following year the same thing happened and Dad took the class for the third time. It happens the theory of Entelev®/Cancell® now Protocel® is bound up in the DeBye Theory and Dr. Jake Warner made sure Dad never forgot it.

A third incident and the one that convinced Dad that he was on the right path occurred while doing research in the library. He had gone to read some bound scientific articles that were printed one after another in the text. As he searched for the correct references he noticed the title of an article, "The Formula" at the bottom of the page followed by the formula which he had seen so often in his dreams. He sat there for quite sometime looking at the words and the formula without turning the page to read the article. He had the feeling that this was an important moment. As he sat there he said to God that if this article referred to cancer he would know he was on the right track. He turned the page and discovered that the formula was that of a carcinogen.

In 1935, Dad went to work for Dow Chemical Company in Midland, Michigan. Previously he had worked as a chemist for a company in Pittsburgh where the secretary was named Estelle Marie

Azinger. Apparently the young chemist was the center of much speculation and attention from the young women employed there. As Dad told it, one Saturday, Estelle asked him if he had eaten his lunch. When he said, "No, why?" She replied, "Well then I think I'll let you take me to lunch." Mom always laughed when Dad told this story but never denied it. Thus, began one of the great romances of all time. In 1935 when Dad made the move to Michigan, he asked Estelle to marry him, but she was fearful of leaving home and a large motherless family that depended on her. Dad went alone. He returned on visits, but finally came the ultimatum. He told Mom he would not be back, he loved her but he had much to do. Fearful that he meant it, Estelle agreed and they were married on December 26, 1936. Their union lasted 64 ½ years. The family eventually grew to five when in 1940 Dennis Michael was born, followed by Margaret Ann and James Edward. I, Marge or Peg as the family calls me, am fond of telling people I am one of the lucky one's who was not brought up in a dysfunctional family. My mother and father were wonderful people whose undying devotion to God, each other, and their children was the glue that held us together. My brothers and I have such wonderful memories of the times spent with our parents and each other.

In September 1936 before the marriage took place, Dad had the dream that brought together all the events of the past. During a nap, he saw the bands of color of the rainbow, which represented the respiratory enzymes. Each color represented an enzyme at a specific redox level. The electrons from the DeBye Theory represented energy units in the respiration moving from glucose to oxygen via the respiratory system. Dad awoke knowing that he had his "Marching Orders." (I would recommend reading an eBooklet by Tanya Harter Pierce available at www.outsmartyourcancer.com for a more detailed explanation of the science.) Three years later, Dad bought his first white mice and began his work mostly at home in his spare time.

"The Project," as the family came to refer to it, was always part of our life. In fact my brother, Dennis, was one of the original recipients of Dad's formula. Dennis had surgery and developed a Keloid Scar. For some reason, it was mother who suggested that they give him Dad's formula to see what would happen to the scar. It went away. I had an even more dramatic demonstration of this when my sister-in-law married a man who had had surgery for a kidney stone. He had the worst Keloid Scar I have ever seen. It looked like a heavy purple rope on his skin and stretched from back to front. When

I told him about Entelev®, he decided to try it. He remained on it for 11 months. Now you can barely tell the scar was ever there but if you look closely you can see a thin silvery line of normal scar tissue.

We children were involved with all aspects of Dad's career and spent countless hours talking about "The Project", working with Dad, praying, sharing Dad's dreams, which were sometimes quite funny in nature, and generally living with "The Project" all the years of our lives. We came to embrace our father's goal to somehow get "Jim's Juice" to the people no matter what obstacles were placed in our path. Dad did not want to personally benefit financially from the knowledge he felt was a gift from God. During his lifetime he gave away the "juice" to those who requested it. Since there was obviously expense associated with such an endeavor, people often helped with fund raisers to pay for chemicals and related items and a foundation, called The Eden Foundation, was set up for donations to buy materials for experiments. The foundation still exists and all monies continue to go to research. Volunteers have always run it. On three different occasions, relatives or friends left money to my mother for her to take a vacation or do something for just herself and each time the money went to "The Project".

During these years the formula had many names. The first we remember was KC49, but for years the family as well as friends referred to it as "Jim's Juice." When Dad decided to name it, he gave it a great deal of thought and came up with Entelev®. He picked the name because he said it referred to the Greek work, Entelechy, which Dad always said meant to him, "That part of man which only God understands."

Probably in the past the "juice" was best known by the name Cancell®. This came about in the 1980's. Through someone Dad knew, an early version of the formula was passed onto a chemist. Through this chemist, a man named Edward Sopcak, a metallurgist, obtained the information. He was very interested in pursuing the work and tried making it himself. He contacted Dad and they began to work together. Mr. Sopcak was a real blessing to Dad and they became friends. He manufactured Entelev® (which he renamed Cancell®) and met with my Dad every two weeks or so for lunch and afternoon meetings to discuss "The Project." They had many discussions on how to tweak the formula to make it more effective. Mr. Sopcak began giving away Cancell® just as Dad had always given away Entelev®. He was often the spokesman for "The Project" during those years. Mr. Sopcak loved to take on the powers that be and challenge them to debate. This left my Dad free to keep a lower profile and concentrate on the chemistry, experimentation and to think. At least that is what Dad always told us he was doing when he **appeared** to be doing nothing.

In the early 1990's, both Dad and Mr. Sopcak's efforts were getting a great deal of attention from the media as well as the government. The National Cancer Institute decided to test the formula and got very positive results. They then sent Dad a letter stating that they did not plan to pursue the matter. I will always remember the shock with which this letter was greeted. Dad sat for days with it in his hand not believing the contents. The test results had been sent to him and he knew the formula had worked. At that time, I was reminded of an incident that took place at a camp where we were vacationing around 1974. All the extended Sheridan Clan met for a week together. I had asked Dad to update me on just what was going on since I lived out of state. As we were talking, he again told me how he had asked God for the knowledge to cure cancer and added that he had also told God that he wanted neither fame nor money from this knowledge. When he said it, I had a physical reaction as a shiver shot down my spine and I felt tightness in my chest. I knew that day that whatever God's plan for Dad's formula, it would not happen during his lifetime on this earth. I do not usually trust my premonitions, but when the letter came from NCI, I knew for sure that this one was true.

My brother, Jim, was very angry about the letter from NCI. He tracked down the doctor who had overseen the tests and asked WHY? The reply was, "Anything that works that good must be too toxic for humans to take." My brother explained it is non-toxic and the response was "Mr. Sheridan has never proven that." That was a fact which could not be disputed. The toxicity test must be run in a FDA approved lab in order to be valid. On three different occasions the tests were contracted for, and then, mysteriously the lab declined to do them. To show how ridiculous things often got, in an earlier experience just when we thought the key had been found to move Dad's work forward, his efforts were rejected because "he could not prove he owned the idea."

In the mid 1990's, Dad's health began to fail and the Sheridan family and Mr. Sopcak decided to separate their efforts, because Sopcak did not agree with how the formula worked and wished to go in the direction of homeopathic medicine and diet. Mr. Sopcak wrote a letter to all those he had supplied with Cancell® stating that Entelev® and

Cancell® were the same and that it belonged to the Sheridans. Meanwhile, Mr. Sopcak was going to pursue homeopathic medicine. Sadly, Mr. Sopcak's health failed not too much later as well. In 2001, Dad and Edward Sopcak died within weeks of each other. I wonder if they are up there discussing how to tweak the formula as in days of yester year. These events left us floundering for a time, but as always we were blessed with friends and family who were interested in "The Project." As someone once said, a good general needs to be surrounded by loyal troops and we have seen many over the years. I would like to mention only a few and thank them. One of the first people to ever get the gift of Entelev® was a friend of Dad's named Chuck Fossati who was suffering from cancer. When Chuck returned to health, he and his wife Mindy bought the pint bottles for Entelev® for many years and provided Dad with an office at their business after he retired from the law firm with which he was associated. (Dad was also a chemical patent attorney who had studied the law and passed the bar during the time he worked for Dow Chemical Company.) Chuck passed away some time ago, but not from cancer. His wife Mindy has remained faithful to "The Project". She is the secretary/treasurer for our group and also the administrator of "The Eden Foundation". The family owes Mindy a great deal. Another friend,

Warren Mertens, who was an accountant, also helped Dad in numerous ways. He was often our calm voice of reason when problems arose. Mr. Mertens passed away in the 1990's. We recently lost another member of our team. His name was Borys Ryzyj. While a pre-med. student, he became interested in Dad's work. He spent many hours sorting papers and organizing thousands of notes made by Dad as well as providing a sounding board for Dad in those last days before his health failed. John Spath and his law firm most particularly his secretary, Traci Jones, have also supported our efforts over the years with help with legal issues.

"The Project" might have ended if it had not been for the efforts of another chemist named Tony Bell. Dr. Bell's brother was another recipient of Entelev®/Cancell® who did very well. Dr. Bell became associated with the family and is now acting as our chemist. He worked with those now manufacturing Protocel® to bring it out as a health aid and has spent countless hours answering questions on the phone for anyone who contacts him. His efforts and dedication also brought us Protocel®/Cancell® Formula (#50). The original Protocel®/Entelev® Formula (#23) is the updated version that Dad and Mr. Sopcak worked on until the late 1980's. However Dr. Bell noted that there was a time when certain conditions reacted better than at other times. He and Borys were able to track down through the help of Ed Sopcak's daughter, Mary, what change was used by Dad and Mr. Sopcak during this time and thus Protocel®/Cancell® Formula (#50) came to be. What formula is recommended depends on each individual's reasons for taking Protocel®. Along with Dr. Bell came his friend and co-worker, Eilert Ofstead, who has also been of a great deal of assistance in furthering our efforts. He helped with the chemistry as well as with computer work and continues to offer sound advice to the family. I would like to add that these people have all acted as volunteers for many years giving of their time and resources to keep James Sheridan's work alive. Not just the family, but the world owes them a great debt.

The family is also grateful to Leanne Breiholz, Jim Sheridan's granddaughter, who has stepped forward from the next generation to help with research and in other ways over the years. It is nice to have the next generation represented. Recently, two other grandchildren, Laura Grove and Anita Sheridan, have joined the organization as volunteers.

I would be remiss if I did not mention two others, both great women, and their husbands who have become such a blessing to "The Project". First, Kathy Buccarrelli who many years ago decided to host a picnic in the Pennsylvania/Ohio area for survivors who had taken and individuals who were taking Entelev®/Cancell® and then Protocel®. This picnic had grown to the point where a hall and a caterer had be hired and people actually traveled from all over the country to attend. It was a place where people could come to meet others, ask questions and get support for their personal situation. The Sheridan family and team thanks you Kathy, and of course, her husband Frank, for all their efforts. Unfortunately, the picnic was suspended a few years ago because Kathy and her husband could no longer host. However, in September of 2009, a Meet-and-Greet was held in Akron, Ohio, with quite a number of people attending.

The other woman is Elonna McKibben. Elonna has shared her own story with so many and has done so much to spread the word about the benefits of Protocel®. I am writing this to be a link on Elonna's latest voluntary effort as she seeks to answer questions for those interested in Protocel® and shares her experience and knowledge about this product. So many people have benefited from

Elonna's dedication to this work and to the support her husband, Rob, has also given to us.

There are many others who have helped along the way that I have not specifically mentioned, but you remain in our hearts and we are grateful for what you all have done. I must thank the fine men who came on board in 2000 and are now the manufacturers of Protocel®. They keep a low profile but are working on "The Project" while also holding down other jobs. Thy have done a lot in the past 10 years and the world has benefited. These are only the latest among the many that have stepped forward in faith to embrace "The Project". Thousands have taken the Entelev®/Cancell®/Protocel® over the years with wonderful results. If this is to live on and become accepted as a treatment, it will be made possible with the help of those people whose lives were affected like Kathy and Frank and Elonna and Rob.

In conclusion, I would like to quote from something my Dad wrote many years ago. I believe it speaks to us all now.

When in the past, people became sick and tired of some nice comfortable government or control group, there came a thing called a revolution. To

143

make further revolution unnecessary, there came a thing called an election. The word election simply means, let's hear the voice of the people....

I can hardly wait to see what form the revolution takes in the present project. I will guess it will be in the form of a "People Injunction"....I hope no one will mind if I enjoy the revolution.

James Vincent Sheridan I always felt this "Project" was on God's timetable. I pray that the revolution has begun.

Saving the Best for the Last!

Our Amazing Healing Discovery

In 2021 I made my most important healing discovery. I wish to share it with you. So here goes.

I began to study artificial intelligence. In reading up on the QFS (quantum financial system) that was just beginning to emerge in the banking system, I found some intriguing and hard-to-believe information. There was plenty of information available about what the QFS would do for mankind (better, faster banking, more honest and dependable system, etc.) there was little or no information about how it worked.

I have a personal rule; if I don't understand it, I avoid it. So I jumped into a quick study to see if I could understand it, since it seemed so important to the future of mankind.

Briefly, what I discovered is that as computers got more and more sophisticated, and faster and faster, and more "intelligent", scientists were reaching the point where they had learned how to interface computers with the human mind. I will not go any further in this explanation, because, frankly, it get freaky and hard-to-believe if you go any deeper.

As I was working my way through all of this, I got some advice in meditation. My spirit guides advised me not to fret because mankind had already been using this technology for a thousand years. They then mentioned the Holy Water used by the Catholic Church.

Years ago, when I practiced Radionics healing extensively, I had, yes, learned that Holy Water does have special healing power. I had actually bought some Holy Water online, placed it in test tube, and had used it as a "reagent" to speed up certain healing processes. In other words, when I added the vibrational qualities of the Holy Water to the vibrations that were being sent to a person's affliction, the healing process was improved. So I knew that Holy Water was special.

I next went to the Internet to learn more about Holy water. Here is how it is made; a group of Priests fill a church fountain or other container with water and then they pray over it. They, in essence, bless the water. Then it becomes Holy Water. Pretty simple.

146

There are 3 prayers that they may use for this process. All are basically the same. Here is one of them:

"Blessed are you, Lord, all-powerful God, who in Christ, the living water of salvation, blessed and transformed us. Grant that when we are sprinkled with this water or make use of it, we will be refreshed inwardly by the power of the Holy Spirit and continue to walk in the new life we received at Baptism."

I was surprised that the simplicity of this prayer. Basically, all it does is commit the water to the wonderful power of God.

Then things got really wonderful and special. This is hard to explain, but I will try my best to explain it to you.

I was told that the water being blessed and prayed over was capable of assisting mankind much more. But it had to be instructed by God to do so. Then the water would directly (in the case of illness), attack and remove the illness. Or in case of emotional distress, remove the harmful emotions and restore the body to happiness and balance.

Basically, this process changes the water in your body from a passive status to a status where it becomes an active healing agent. It was emphatically stressed that, unless the water as asked by God to do this, it would not work.

Where an understanding of Artificial Intelligence comes in

If you ponder on this for a while, as I have done, things become more clear. Artificial Intelligence involves establishing a link with the human mind and a non-human object (the computer). This link goes through God. God somehow allows this link (information) to be passed on to other mechanisms in God's realm, and the work is done. Not a great explanation, but is the best that I can offer, given my own limitations.

Well, the same basic thing happens with Holy Water. I have explained this in other sections of my book "On Stormy Seas". The written works of Viktor Shauberger and Masaru Emoto delve sufficiently into water's ability to carry conscience and intelligence.

Thus when the Priests pray over the water, they impart a request that God bless the water with their message. God does this, and from then on the water has special curative powers. The water then later passes this curative power on to you.

So my Spirit Guides are right. The enlightenment of our knowledge of artificial intelligence does lead us right back to the knowledge of Holy Water that has been known for a thousand years. Interesting.

Where are we going with this?

I have to be careful here, as I do not wish to inadvertently reveal anything that I am not supposed to reveal.

What my Spiritual Advisors have told me is to take the basic prayer to bless Holy Water and "soup" it up by asking the water to do extra things, which it will most probably be happy to do for you and God. Remember always that God is approving everything, so you cannot inadvertently ask for anything that goes against God's will. Should you accidently do so, it is simple. God will not grant your request.

So, my first chance to use this knowledge came when two of my beloved Essiac employees got sick from taking Covid vaccinations shots. They drank this water. They immediately got better. I have also been using this knowledge to improve my own health and well as helping my wife deal with some health issues. It is working for us. I am going to list here several of the requests that we have been using.

Dear God, Please instruct this water to remove all harmful substances from my body. Please remove all illness and disease from my body. Please remove all harm from the Covid and the Covid vaccinations. Thank you. We love you.	**Dear God, Please instruct the water in my body to restore my energy levels to that of a 35 year-old person. Thank you and I love you.**
Dear God, Please instruct this water to heal And cure the swelling in my feet And legs. Thank you. I love you.	Dear God, Please instruct this water to remove the excess and unhealthy fat from my body And restore my body shape to a healthy Condition. I love you. Thank you.

Using Energy Plates to assist us

Here is the system that I use; I use a credit card sized energy plate. I buy mine at purpleplates.com. These aluminum plates are imbued with life force energy. I have used them successfully for many years for other healing purposes. I then perform a consecration ritual where I pass the message for my healing to the energy plate, all the while asking God to approve everything. I then print the prayer request, cut it out, ask God to bless it (through a prayer) and tape it to the energy plate. I cover everything in plastic. I then take this energy plate and tape it or fasten it to the water pipe feeding the faucet where I draw my drinking and cooking water. Sometimes, depending on the complexity of the house water piping system, I just fasten the plate to the cold water line that feeds the house (usually near the water heater).

Thus the blessed message is passed on to the water that I drink. The water does the rest. Some people prefer to carry the energy plate in their pocket. Either method works.

After a while you may get your own inspiration on various ways to use this information. Just be sure to get God's permission.

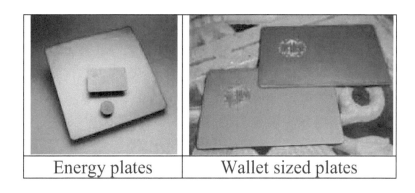

| Energy plates | Wallet sized plates |

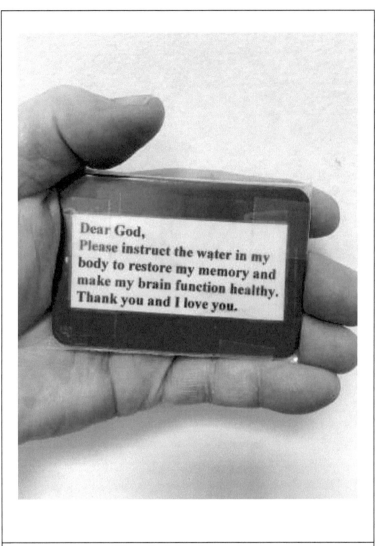

The finished product

Let's all stay young and healthy!

ADDENDUMS

Special Bonus Section

Additional Information for our Inquisitive Readers

Do you know anyone who has skin cancer? If so, you may wish to show them this information. This inexpensive cream really works!

Our "Super Dooper" Skin Cancer Salve

There are two ingredients in our "Super Dooper" skin cancer salve:

Hydrogen Peroxide.

The main ingredient is liquid hydrogen peroxide. It is not just any-old drug store variety of peroxide. It is a special kind of hydrogen peroxide that is labeled **"35% Food Grade Hydrogen Peroxide"**.

This special peroxide can be found at many health food stores, or it can be bought online.

The last 16 oz. bottle that I bought cost me about $20.00. It will last me about 6 months.

35% Food Grade Hydrogen Peroxide

How it works.

The chemical expression for hydrogen peroxide is H_2O_2. When the hydrogen peroxide is placed on your skin, it transfers to H_2O (water) and O (a free molecule of oxygen). This free molecule of oxygen is very reactive. It wants to quickly bond with something else.

If the hydrogen peroxide has been placed on a malignant tumor (such as a skin cancer tumor) it will quickly bond with the tumor.

But the cancerous tumor is anaerobic; it cannot exist in the presence of oxygen. Thus it immediately dies.

And that, dear friend is how it works. It works fast. It is simple to apply. And, in my many years of using this salve, I have never failed to see it work properly.

A few words of caution.

Hydrogen peroxide is very sensitive to light. If it is not stored in a dark place, it will deteriorate quickly. It should be kept is a light- proof bottle, and the bottle should be stored in a cool, dark place.

Also, it should be replaced every year-or-so. Age will reduce its strength.

Aloe Vera Gel.

The other ingredient is aloe vera gel.

Aloe Vera Gel

This is easier to obtain. You can find it at almost any drug store, grocery store, or health food store. A 16 oz. bottle or jar costs me about $16.00.

Making the Salve:

Making the salve is incredibly easy. Just mix up the amount that you will need. Make the ration about 50% peroxide and 50% aloe vera gel. It is that simple.

You may want to use a plastic, wood or metal spoon for your mixing, as the 35% peroxide is very strong and may burn your fingers.

Store your salve in a light-proof bottle and keep in in a dark place (a refrigerator works fine).

Using the Salve:

Apply the salve to your skin cancer as needed. The more you apply, the faster it will act.

If, when you apply the salve, you see a bubbling action, this is a really good sign. The bubbling action is the active oxygen molecule in the peroxide mixing with the cancerous growth.

You should see results within a few days.

Note: This information is extracted from the book **"The Skin Cancer Information Handbook"** by Michael D. Miller.

Another Bonus Chapter!

Explaining Where Sacred Geometry Came From: A Fable Story

I am presenting the following information as a fable. Why a fable? Because I cannot prove to you that it is true. But, like many fables, some people believe that it is true. Including me. This fable is put together from 40 years of reading, meditation, studies, and pondering. So I am offering it to you for your amusement/consideration.

By virtue of your open-mindedness that you have shown in reading this book, I am assuming that some of you may appreciate this information. It is offered to you in the spirit of friendship and appreciation for reading my book. Let's "fable" onward.

About Sacred Geometry: In order to explain where it is that sacred geometry and the concepts and knowledge of how to harness the powers of sacred geometry came from, we first have to delve into the matter of how mankind was created.

Most of our knowledge here is offered to us from the bible. But the bible was written two thousand years ago, during a time when most people were illiterate and uneducated. So the written stories in the bible of our creation may have served well two thousand years ago. But today we seek better and more complete knowledge.

Thus it is that stories such as this are written.

Zachariah Sitchin

As a quick introduction, here is how Wikipedia explains this man:

Zechariah Sitchin (July 11, 1920 – October 9, 2010)[1] was an author of a number of books proposing an explanation for human origins involving ancient astronauts. Sitchin attributed the creation of the ancient Sumerian culture to the Anunnaki, which he stated was a race of extraterrestrials from a planet beyond Neptune called Nibiru. He asserted that Sumerian mythology suggests that this hypothetical planet of Nibiru is in an elongated, 3,600-year-long elliptical orbit around the Sun. Sitchin's books have sold millions of copies worldwide and have been translated into more than 25 languages.

Many years ago I began to read the books written by this famous anthropologist Zachariah Sitchin. He was said to be the only person who could read the ancient Sumerian hieroglyphic clay tablets and scrolls.

His writing were different, they were provocative. Few experts agreed with him. But he stated some very important things, things that made sense. Things that meshed with other facts of the scientific community.

As I checked him out, I found that he really was the only scientist in the world who could read the ancient Sumerian hieroglyphics. These ancient clay tablets were from antiquity. And Mr. Sitchin drew much of his information from them. A prolific writer, he wrote about 12 books, all based on information from analysis of the Sumerian clay tablets. He told the creation of man story from a different perspective, a different viewpoint. And his stories were interesting! So I, over the years, read many of his books.

Then I hit pay dirt. Just before he retired, he published the book **"The Lost Book of Enki"**. It told the story of mankind's creation, as seen through the eyes of several of the ancient Alien beings that had inhabited earth. They had created mankind to use as a slave race to help them mine the abundant gold deposits that they found on earth.

His story really made sense to me. His story, as always, was based on information that he had gleaned from the ancient Sumerian hieroglyphics. It was consistent with the bible, and all known information about our creation.

Mr. Sitchin has since passed away. But his information made a big impression on me, and gave me a newly expanded knowledge about how we were created.

Then a fascinating guy by the name of Clif High also published a report about the creation of mankind. It meshed perfectly with the material presented by Zachariah Sitchin. Plus it gave an interesting insight into how the Egyptian Mystery Schools were created, and where the information taught in the Egyptian Mystery Schools came from.

What was Zachariah Sitchin's Information about Creation? Here, in a nutshell, is what Mr. Sitchin told us in his book *The Lost Book of Enki*:

1. A group of Aliens known as the Anunnaki came to earth eons ago. They were searching for gold, a mineral scarce on their own planet.
2. They found plenty of gold on earth.
3. They were not a race of beings that were used to doing labor. Therefore they attempted to mine gold using the local beings that they found on earth.
4. This did not work. The local people were also not good workers.
5. They set about to clone a new race of beings who would be good workers (miners).

6. They developed a cloned being that was made up of beings from the planet Sirius, with strands of DNA added to "dumb them down" to make them controllable workers. The added strands (2 strands) of DNA were from a reptilian source.
7. This new cloned being was a successful venture. Gold mining progressed.
8. The new beings multiplied and became numerous.
9. Eventually the Anunnaki decided to return to their home, the planet Niburu.
10. They arranged for the Great Flood that would destroy their cloned worker society.
11. Some enlightened Anunnaki objected to the destruction of the worker society, they interfered, and thus some of mankind survived the deluge.
12. And thus we were created to eventually multiply and cover the earth.

My interesting observation: The Sirians were a pure race of people, very spiritual and honest. When the cloners added two strands of reptilian DNA to the Sirian body, they created good

Zachariah Sitchin

workers for their mines. But they also had
introduced into our being a capacity for evil that
the Sirians did not have.

I find this information consistent with many writing that discuss God and his plan for mankind. Many see that God's plan is for us to overcome this tendency toward evil that was bred into mankind. When we have finally overcome this handicap, we will all joyfully return to be with God forever. We will be experienced "warriors" who have fought the good fight and have triumphantly returned to the God that loves us so much!

Anyway, let us now look at the story of mankind's creation as told by my guru Clif High.

Clif High's story of creation

About Clif High: For over 14 years I have been a fan of Clif High. He first made a name for himself by developing a method for extracting predictions from the language patterns of mankind. He was hired by major corporations to utilize his information. He eventually retired to the woods of

Washington state, where he pumps out a very interesting newsletter.

I have found his information sincere and truthful. An article written by him follows:

This colony, Earth.
We've been invaded by Space Aliens!

This Colony, Earth.

We've been invaded by Space Aliens

Six thousand years ago, more or less, Earth was invaded by Space Aliens.

They came down all around the planet, in the lands just north of the Tropic of Cancer. The Space Alien invasion arrived in a small, but heavily armed, force, with the clear intent to conquer and colonize Earth.

They landed in Yucatan Peninsula. They landed in Macedonia, Sumer, India, China, and Japan, and elsewhere.

From these bases, their superior technology which included over 40 different types of flying war machines, they easily conquered the hunter-gatherer tribes inhabiting the area.

In each area thus conquered, the local tribes provided the name for the Space Aliens in their own language. Thus we know the Colonists as the Elohim, the Devas, the Theoae, the Anunnaki, the Shin, and in all cases, in all languages those names became synonymous with 'gods'.

Once the local tribes were conquered, the Space Aliens conscripted their local human population to go forth, and conquer other, more distant tribes of humans. They did so, with the occasional assistance of the Space Alien 'lords'.

As the combat local to the landing sites faded away, the Space Alien overlords set about building vast complexes on the conquered territory. These were called GANS in their language, which our religious texts today, translate as 'gardens'.

Clif High, Internet Guru, developer of "Predictive Linguistics"

These GANS were the Space Alien's genetic material production laboratories. These GANS had 'energy shields' which prevented non-authorized access by the local populations of humans. It is thought now that the GANS enclosed several hundreds of square kilometers of area, rising several thousands of feet. These energy shields also provided both air, and light filtration.

The Space Alien overlords needed both. The light had to be moderated due to their biological needs for reduced levels of cosmic radiation of all forms. The air needed to be sterilized as it flowed into the GANS because the Space Aliens were vulnerable to earth bacteria to an extreme level.

As the GANS were stabilized, the Space Alien scientists and production crews came down to Colony Earth, and set to work. Their goal was to create a smart-enough, but not too smart, slave species.

The work in the GANS continued for approximately 2000 years.

It was difficult work, building an effective slave species from the local genetic base merged with part of the genetic material of the Space Alien Colonists. There were many wrong choices made, and species were created, then destroyed when they did not meet specifications. Some, including the Giants, escaped the GANS to roam about the land, but as these beings were engineered, and not native to this environment, they failed to thrive, all eventually succumbing to adverse conditions.

About 4000 years ago, a certain level of success in the engineering of the Colonists was achieved with the creation of the first of the 'white people'. Variously, the Space Aliens had already, from the native brown humans, created Black, Yellow, Red, and then finally White people.

It was difficult work, and it would seem that the Space Alien Colonists stopped their genetic engineering with the creation of the white people. It is not known if this was due to their goal being achieved, or if external, adverse circumstances altered the direction of the Space Alien overlords' efforts.

Shortly after their successful engineering of their slave species, the Space Alien Colonists left earth.

We don't know, for sure, why they left.

There are hints, in our ancient literature, that rising cosmic radiation levels created conditions on Earth that greatly increased the risk to the Space Alien Colonists in the form of bacterial infection. The Space Alien overloads were very long lived, especially when protected by the filtration of the energy shields around the GANS. It is thought that they lived many thousands of years, perhaps, in a protected environment, into the 10's of thousands of years. Though the Colonists were protected, and long lived, they were acutely afraid of death.

Out in the wild, that is, in the unprotected areas of Colony Earth, the Space Alien Colonists had need of extraordinary precautions to avoid bacterial infections of which, even minor ones were rapidly fatal.

About 4000 years ago, conditions changed here on Earth for the Colonists, and they left. The leaving was a mass exodus that was completed in a remarkably short period of time.

It is speculated that there was some level of failure of the GANS energy shields that prompted the Space Alien Colonists to flee.

The failure, and removal of the GANS structures allowed the engineered slave species the freedom to walk the Earth. As an engineered species, and non-native to this environment, the created Humans struggled to survive, though, they were successful.

It greatly aided the newly liberated slave species that the food stock animals and plants built by the Colonists to feed their slaves were very hardy within the Earth's biosphere, spreading across the lands.

When the Space Alien Colonists left Earth, the managerial class of slaves, who were the go-between for the Space Aliens in their interaction with their created slave species, moved in to fill the power vacuum.

At that time, there was a concerted effort on the part of the managerial class of slaves to claim the power that had been held by the Space Alien Colonists.

The managers declared themselves a 'priest' class, moved the now absent Space Alien Overlords from a status of physical beings into a category of 'transcendent omnipotent invisible gods', and declared that they, the priests, were the only ones with 'authority', both here on Earth, over other members of the slave species, as well as with the intercession process of communication with the Space Alien overlords.

It was a sweet gig for the priest class. Too good, too soft & cushy of a position, to easily surrender. Thus the many ills associated with the implementation of religion can be seen to arise from these circumstances.

As also may be inferred, thus arose the human practice of Colonization, of War, as we practice it, of Law as it pertains to interactions between ourselves, and many, many other attributes of our lives here, in this resulting, now.

Civilization, as we know it now, is not a human invention. It was impressed upon the engineered descendants of the original hunter-gatherer tribes by the invading Colonists, both by pressure of force, and by cultural mimicry of the newly formed humans adopting the superior ways of the Space Alien Colonists over the tribal forms of their precedents who provided the base biological source for their genetics.

There have been other civilizations here on Earth. They existed prior to the coming of the Space Alien Colonists.

There have been other, modern humans, here on Earth, who built those civilizations. We are separated from them by the Great Ice Age.

Our antecedents, those hunter-gatherer tribes, were themselves a remnant of the previous ages of Humans, here on Earth. If it had not been for the impact of the Great Ice upon the previous Age of Man here on Earth, the Space Alien Colonists might not have had such an easy time of it with our ancestors.

Though the priest class will maintain that the Space Alien Colonists 'created' modern humans in their GANS laboratories, do not be deceived. The Space Aliens are not gods, they are tinkerers. They made small tweaks in humanity, they did not create us. Their goal was to make us just-smart-enough, and docile.

It did not quite work. Humans are far smarter than the Colonists wanted, and not close enough to docile to be able to be controlled, as our priest class is constantly complaining. Perhaps this contributed to the Exodus. Maybe, when we get our species collective ass out into space, and we find these Space Alien Colonists, we can ask them.

Clif High

My Summary and Conclusions about the Anunnaki and our knowledge of Sacred Geometry

The Anunnaki had created their "worker race" who would do their mining for them on earth. In the process of organizing this work force, it was necessary to have some of these workers be supervisors in order to direct the rest of the workers.

Thus it was, in the thousands of years that followed, a separate level or "Order of Supervisors" was established. They were ranked as superior to the worker force, but were, of course, lower than the lowest Anunnaki supervisors.

Then, eventually, the decision to abandon earth had been made. Enki and his friends had taken steps to insure that some of their "worker force" had survived the deluge that was set upon the earth to destroy the workers (the legend of Noah and his ark?). Then the Anunnaki left earth, leaving the surviving workers to fend for themselves. Some of these surviving workers were of the Supervisor class.

These surviving Survivor class workers had, though their closer contact with the Anunnaki, learned much of the Anunnaki wisdom and knowledge. Because the Supervisors had superior knowledge and information, it was easy for them to establish themselves as the new ruling class. This morphed into them becoming the Religious or Priestly Class who ruled over the more-ordinary masses.

Among this knowledge of the Priestly Class was knowledge of the principles of sacred geometry, and how the Anunnaki had utilized this knowledge to enhance their lives and work.

As Priestly classes tend to do, they did not share their esoteric knowledge with the masses. They hoarded this information in order to increase their power over the masses. Thus it was, that with time, arcane knowledge of things such as sacred geometry, was only known by a special group of the Priestly Class (I will hereinafter refer to them as the "Priests").

With this as a background, mankind began his sojourn on earth.

God took advantage of this situation. He set up a plan to enrich the knowledge and wisdom of select angels.

God sent these angels to live on the earth as men, and to begin the long and difficult path to attaining enlightenment. They had to overcome the challenges offered here on earth. These challenges were due to the reptilian strands in our bodies that gave us a capacity for evil. When we have overcome the challenges that are found here on earth (i.e., having overcome our capacity for evil), we will once again be reunited with God. This is God's plan for us. It is a great plan.

When we have won our struggle and have returned to God we will be wiser and more enlightened. We will, in short, be more godlike. His love for us, and our love for Him, will be increased immensely. We will be Super Angels. This is his gift to us. Yes, it is a great plan.

For thousands of years the powers of sacred geometry existed, but most of mankind didn't know about it. So as we now progress onward, knowledge of things such as sacred geometry is coming to us. It comes in bits and pieces, but it comes. This perhaps means that it is time for us to relearn this ancient knowledge. Perhaps that is why you are reading this book.

Some More Special Bonus Addendum

Pyramid Power
How to shave for almost free!

My dad was an interesting guy. Raised on a farm in Minnesota during the Depression, he didn't have an opportunity to get an education. But he was smart, and had an inquiring mind. He read a lot.

So back in the 1970's he sent me a book titled "Pyramid Power". Interesting book, it elaborated on the special powers of a pyramid built with the geometric ratios of the Great Pyramid of Egypt. In the book, it stated that if you placed a shaving razor at a point 1/3 down from the apex of the pyramid, that the razor would stay sharp.

Many years later, I remembered this. So when I was experimenting with some small replicas of the Great Pyramid, I tried this experiment. It worked. For years I kept my shaving razor sharp with this method. But it was awkward because of the difficulty in keeping a pyramid structure in the vicinity of my bathroom. The smallest pyramid that I could fine to use was about 24 inches wide and 19 inches tall. There was never enough space in my bathroom to use the device. So I gradually stopped using it.

Here is what I learned: I could use an ordinary disposable razor. Normally such a razor would stay sharp for about a week, then had to be thrown away. I could place it under the apex of the pyramid. And then it lasted me for up to six months. Pretty neat. But as I mentioned, it was very inconvenient to use because of the bulky size of the pyramid.

Well friends, I have just made another discovery that I wish to share with you. I have found a very small brass pyramid that works well to keep my razor sharp. The brass pyramid is only 2 inches square, so it fits on my bathroom shelf nicely. And I bought it on the Internet for less than $10.00. I placed my razor (shown in the picture) on the apex of the pyramid as shown. I started using this disposable razor in January of this year. It is now August, and the razor is a sharp as it was on the first day I used it (maybe even sharper).

Here is a picture of my rig:

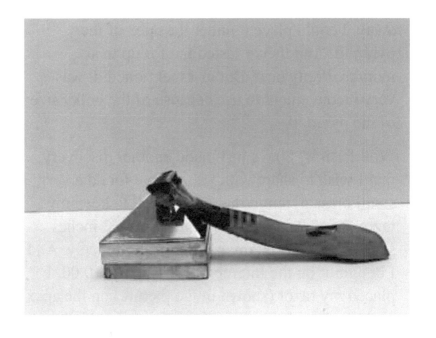

In case any of you wish to experiment with this rig, you can google "small brass pyramid". Mine came as a set of 3 pyramids. I stacked them as shown in the photo for maximum power.

As I mentioned before, the set of 3 small brass pyramids cost me around $10.00. Then the razor cost me about $3.00. If they last for a year, my total cost of shaving for the year will be $13.00. Not bad! And I still have the pyramids!

By the way, here is a list of books that I have written (some with pen names). They are available on amazon.com.

On Stormy Seas	Elk Hunting Guide
Increasing Your Cat's Life & Longevity	Kill Zone
Increasing Your Dog's Longevity	Egyptian Sacred Geometry
The Lyme Disease Handbook	Pirate History of Florida
Women's Beauty Secrets	Essiac Story and 6 Examples
Defending Against the Ambush	Two Essiac Angels
The Diabetes Handbook	Essiac Handbook
Salt and Your Health	Essiac Testimonials
Structured Water for Greater Health and Happiness	A Terrible Beauty
	Sacred Geometry Healing Water
	Male Menopause

| Greater Longevity; Rediscovering the Philosopher's Stone | Women's Health Secrets

Beating Arthritis |
|---|---|
| | |

Made in United States
Troutdale, OR
01/27/2024

17193309R00106